Testing Tolerance

MASTER CLASS: RESOURCES FOR TEACHING MASS COMMUNICATION

Series Editor: Chris Roush

Other books in the series:
Master Class: Teaching Advice for Journalism and Mass Communication Instructors edited by Chris Roush

About AEJMC:
The Association for Education in Journalism and Mass Communication (AEJMC) is a nonprofit organization of more than 3,700 educators, students, and practitioners from around the globe. Founded in 1912 by Willard Grosvenor Bleyer, the first president (1912–1913) of the American Association of Teachers of Journalism, as it was then known, AEJMC is the oldest and largest alliance of journalism and mass communication educators and administrators at the college level.

AEJMC's mission is to promote the highest possible standards for journalism and mass communication education, to encourage the widest possible range of communication research, to encourage the implementation of a multicultural society in the classroom and curriculum, and to defend and maintain freedom of communication in an effort to achieve better professional practice, a better informed public, and wider human understanding.

About the Series Editor:
Chris Roush is the Walter E. Hussman Sr. Distinguished Professor in Business Journalism at University of North Carolina-Chapel Hill. In 2010, he was named Journalism Teacher of the Year by the Scripps Howard Foundation and the Association for Education in Journalism and Mass Communication. The judges noted that Roush "has become the expert in business journalism—not just at Chapel Hill, but throughout the country and even in other parts of the world." He has also been named the North Carolina Professor of the Year by the Carnegie Foundation for the Advancement of Teaching and Council for Advancement and Support of Education.

Testing Tolerance

Addressing Controversy in the Journalism and Mass Communication Classroom

AEJMC Commission on the Status of Women

Edited by
Candi Carter Olson, Utah State University
Tracy Everbach, University of North Texas

aejmc

Published in partnership with the Association for
Education in Journalism and Mass Communication
Commission on the Status of Women
ROWMAN & LITTLEFIELD
Lanham • Boulder • New York • London

Published in partnership with the Association for Education in Journalism and Mass Communication Commission on the Status of Women

Published by Rowman & Littlefield
An imprint of The Rowman & Littlefield Publishing Group, Inc.
4501 Forbes Boulevard, Suite 200, Lanham, Maryland 20706
www.rowman.com

6 Tinworth Street, London SE11 5AL, United Kingdom

British Library Cataloguing in Publication Information Available

Library of Congress Cataloging-in-Publication Data
Names: Carter Olson, Candi S., 1977– editor. | Everbach, Tracy, 1962– editor.
Title: Testing tolerance : addressing controversy in the journalism and mass communication classroom / edited by Candi Carter Olson, Utah State University ; Tracy Everbach, University of North Texas.
Description: Lanham : Rowman & Littlefield, 2020. | Series: Master class: resources for teaching mass communication | "AEJMC Commission on the Status of Women." | Includes bibliographical references and index. |
Identifiers: LCCN 2019057336 (print) | LCCN 2019057337 (ebook) | ISBN 9781538132678 (cloth) | ISBN 9781538132692 (epub)
Subjects: LCSH: Journalism—Study and teaching (Higher)—United States. | Communication—Study and teaching (Higher)—United States. | Toleration—Study and teaching (Higher)—United States. | Prejudices—Study and teaching (Higher)—United States.
Classification: LCC PN4788 .T47 2020 (print) | LCC PN4788 (ebook) | DDC 070.071173—dc23
LC record available at https://lccn.loc.gov/2019057336
LC ebook record available at https://lccn.loc.gov/2019057337

Contents

PART II: Fostering Tolerance

1

Introduction

Testing Tolerance in the Classroom

Tracy Everbach and Candi Carter Olson

The headlines are inescapable, whether on social media, online, print, or television:

"Jeffrey Epstein: The Women Accused of Finding Girls for Him"
"Joe Biden: Racism Is Institutional and 'White Man's Problem'"
"Police Are Now Leading Cause of Death among Young American Men"
"Researchers Claim Facebook Ads Could Out LGBTQ+ Users"
"Mom Thanks United for Helping Son with Autism on Flight"

For journalism and mass communication instructors, these headlines can seem particularly overwhelming because they're not only the news, they're also our jobs. Our students read these headlines and refer to them in class. These discussions can lead to many opportunities for free speech, student biases, instructor biases, and learning, which all intersect, and sometimes explode, on college campuses.

How do we handle these discussions as college and university instructors? We shouldn't simply deflect them. We certainly wouldn't in newsrooms.

This book takes the inescapable and makes it accessible for journalism and mass communication college and university instructors. Through a range of perspectives and ideas, this book tackles controversial topics and gives advice for navigating the deep waters surrounding them in formative ways for both students and instructors.

NOT A NEW PHENOMENON

Tackling tough topics is not a new issue for journalism and mass communication classes, although many people point to U.S. president Donald Trump's 2016 election as a spark for current conversations.

Still, the conflicts happening now have been occurring for decades. As experienced journalism and mass communication instructors, we've been leading these types of hot-button discussions for years, first in professional newsrooms and then in classrooms.

We've followed the women's movement's calls to awareness about sexual assault and harassment, from Anita Hill and Monica Lewinsky in the 1990s, when landmark legislation against sexual harassment in the workplace was also passed, to today's takedown of powerful men by #MeToo. Before that, women were actively fighting sexual harassment and assault in the workplace. Eleanor Holmes Norton, the first woman to chair the Equal Employment Opportunity Commission, used her position to push through changes that made sexual harassment a violation of women's rights, and three court cases in the 1970s "confirmed that a woman could sue her employer for harassment under Title VII of the 1964 Civil Rights Act, using the EEOC as the vehicle for redress" (Cohen, 2016, para. 8–9). Successful racial discrimination cases encouraged Black women who were survivors of sexual harassment and assault to press their own cases through the courts, and Black women became leaders in the fight for women's equality at work.

We can point to several U.S. Supreme Court cases on teachers' First Amendment rights to show that instructors have been introducing discourse on important community issues for decades. Their right to do so is important to free speech rights and freedom of ideas in a democracy. In 1969, the Supreme Court wrote in *Tinker v. Des Moines Independent Community School District* that "it can hardly be argued that either students or teachers shed their constitutional rights of freedom of speech or expression at the schoolhouse gate." This tenet is vital for professors to remember because First Amendment rights to honest and open debate can make classroom conversation richer, even as there is more controversy and potential for pitfalls.

While contentious topics consistently have been part of public debate, the 2016 election intensified classroom atmospheres. Combined with the free-for-all of social media and a president who uses Twitter to insult and demean those who disagree with him, those he doesn't like, and worse, vulnerable populations such as immigrants, classrooms more than ever need educators who can lead intense dialogue. College campuses since 2016 have seen white supremacist groups march with tiki torches, swastikas painted on walls, "street preachers" yelling at students and telling them they are going to hell, armed students posing at a plaque marking the lynching of Emmett Till, and nooses found hanging on trees. These types of incidents also occurred in the past, but they have been intensified by a divided political climate in the United States.

To add to the anxious and sometimes antagonistic tone, mass shootings have increased, all while several states have passed laws allowing guns on campus. Both editors of this book teach in states that currently allow concealed carry of handguns in classrooms. Both of us have spent considerable amounts of time undergoing active shooter training, worrying about students who might feel frightened or vulnerable, scanning our lecture halls for anyone who might seem "off" or disturbed—all activities that have taken time, energy, and resources from the educational experiences of our students.

The social chaos of tough topics can cause real pain among students. Sixty-eight percent of Generation Z, our current generation of students, reports feeling very or somewhat stressed about the current state of our nation, including mass shootings, suicide, climate change, immigration, and sexual assault and harassment (McClennen, 2019, paras. 8–11).

> While it may well be true that the era of trigger warnings and safe spaces demands tough conversations about the degree to which a college student should feel safe on campus, there remains little doubt that the pressures these kids face are systemic, structural and certainly not all in their head. (McClennen, 2019, para. 37)

Discussing tough topics in the classroom allows students an outlet to explore their worlds in a safe space and a place where they can vent frustrations about contemporary society. Talking about these issues prepares them to be better citizens of a democratic society, particularly if they're allowed to participate freely. "The nature of democratic life is disagreement and contention, and college campuses, where we shape the leaders of the next generation, are places where disagreements come into sharp focus" (Covaleskie, 2019, p. 2).

Covaleskie (2019) also argues that universities have a responsibility to create safe spaces for historically marginalized groups and need to "actively place themselves on the side of victims of systems of oppression" (p. 3). Openly talking about difficult concepts in our culture is one way to do this. However, many barriers hinder professors' abilities to hold open classroom conversations about threatening or contentious subjects.

TEACHING AMID BIAS

Academia exists in a liminal space, stuck between the historical values of the academy that prize open conversations and in-depth examination of issues and overt criticism and active attempts to defund universities for

those exact same values. Attacks on professors and universities are being driven by social media rage machines. These assaults, Isaac Kamola
(2019) argues, happen in a clear pattern.

> Most attacks are leveled against faculty of color, or those whose research and
> teaching focuses on issues of race. Most start with a handful of organizations
> explicitly created to monitor and intimidate college faculty . . . from there
> they travel to sympathetic right-wing websites and news outlets. . . . Most
> attacks that gain traction involve college administration sanctioning faculty
> and condemning their speech. (Kamola, 2019, p. 3–4)

This punitive cycle has a chilling effect on faculty speech and the approaches that professors take to their classrooms and student work.

Student evaluations as currently implemented also curb faculty speech
and approaches to tough topics in the classroom, particularly if the professor is a woman or minority. Dozens of studies have shown that student
evaluations of teaching are biased negatively against women, people of
color, and international faculty members (Falkoff, 2018; Flaherty, 2019a;
Lawrence, 2018; Vasey & Carroll, 2016). An American Association of
University Professors (AAUP) survey of more than nine thousand faculty
members across the country found that low numbers of students complete evaluations, making validity questionable, and that students often
include comments that have nothing to do with teaching and learning
(Vasey & Carroll, 2016).

> Numerous reports indicated that the abusive and bullying tone often seen in
> anonymous online comments is beginning to appear in student evaluations.
> Some women faculty members and faculty members of color report receiving
> negative comments on appearance and qualifications; it seems that anonym-
> ity may encourage such inappropriate and sometimes overtly discriminatory
> comments. (para. 9)

Many institutions rely inordinately on student ratings of professors to
judge tenure, promotion, raises, and other measures, even though they
have been proven discriminatory. In September 2019, the American Sociological Association, American Historical Association, and sixteen other
professional academic organizations called on universities to stop relying
on student evaluations alone to determine teaching effectiveness (Flaherty, 2019b). The associations noted that such evaluations are problem-
atic and should be considered among a holistic assessment of teaching.

Knowing that students are going to rate them, instructors may be reluctant to confront controversial topics in the classroom. This project aims
to help them find approaches to walking a delicate balance of keeping
the peace while also addressing issues directly. But we also urge faculty

members to fight within their departments, schools, colleges, and universities for more holistic assessments of teaching, such as peer observations, teaching philosophies, teaching portfolios, and other approaches that relegate student evaluations as only one part of a faculty member's teaching ability.

THE EMOTIONAL TOLL ON STUDENTS AND FACULTY

Discussing highly emotional topics is bound to have an effect on both students and instructors. For instance, one of us showed a documentary that ended with footage of the driver who killed Heather Heyer during the 2017 white supremacist rally in Charlottesville, Virginia. Some students became visibly upset, some crying. A student dropped the class, saying it was too much for her to bear.

The pressure also can take a toll on instructors. Teaching tough topics can put professors at odds with students and administrators. The corporatization of the academy has put more focus on professors teaching material that gets students jobs, rather than challenging their thinking and pushing them to think critically. An article in the *Guardian* notes:

> The pressure to satisfy increasing student expectations has fallen on teaching staff. Managers have increased their demands on the academic workforce over concern about university rankings and league tables. At the same time, repeated research and teaching audits have created a culture of workplace surveillance.
>
> Academics are inherently vulnerable to overwork and self-criticism, but the sources of stress have multiplied to the point where many are at a breaking point. (Weale, 2019, paras. 8–9)

Professors who choose to do public intellectual work via social media and mainstream media sources have found themselves under attack for their positions on issues, and some have been fired for saying the wrong thing in the wrong venue. That wrong venue could be the classroom, as increasing surveillance makes the classroom a space that's seemingly open for public scrutiny. For example, since 2016, Turning Point USA, a group dedicated to limited government and free markets, has compiled a "Professor Watch List" of higher education instructors it claims, according to its website, "discriminate against conservative students, promote anti-American values and advance leftist propaganda in the classroom." Some conservative organizations and individuals have accused universities of "indoctrinating" students to leftist thought, rather than assuming that students are drawing their own conclusions based on evidence and learning to consider different viewpoints. Turning Point and other groups have targeted classes that introduce topics like feminism, critical race theory, and social construction of reality (Phillips-Fein, 2019).

Still, tough topics need to be addressed, both in the classroom and publicly on our campuses. This book brings together leading voices in journalism and mass communication education to discuss how to approach tough topics in a variety of venues, from the classroom to administrative offices to public spaces, such as social media. Through this conversation, this book seeks to give journalism and mass communication instructors a toolbox to guide their challenging and rewarding work leading discussions across many stages of their careers.

HOW THE BOOK IS ORGANIZED

Part I begins with chapter 2, by Candi Carter Olson, and covers media literacy and its importance in talking about race, class, gender, disability, sexuality, and other differences. This chapter walks readers through three exercises, each increasing in the discomfort students may feel, and recommends ways to help students through the exercises. Through this discussion, readers will find real-life tools to help them navigate tricky terrain with their students, all while negotiating the potential mental health issues inherent in teaching tough topics and other pushback that professors may encounter from students.

In chapter 3, Tracy Everbach focuses on how to manage controversy and conflict in the classroom. She has been teaching a class on race and gender in the media for more than a decade and offers answers to the question, how do we discuss highly emotional personal and political topics in a civil, intellectual manner? She provides advice on how to lay the groundwork for such discussions and how to handle specific types of difficult situations that may arise.

In chapter 4, Meredith Clark offers strategies to manage the emotional labor faculty of color often face on primarily white campuses. She discusses the invisible labor involved in supporting students and fighting for social justice while completing the everyday work expected of tenure-track professors. She also gives tips on how to keep track of this work and include it in annual evaluation reports and tenure and promotion documents.

Chapter 5 offers readers real classroom advice for navigating the increasing mental health issues that both students and faculty across college campuses are experiencing. Chelsea Reynolds leads readers through her proactive approach to mental health in the classroom. She shares exercises she uses with her students to help them monitor their own sleep, work, and play schedules, emphasizing the importance of a human element in the classroom. Since 95 percent of college counseling center directors report growing concerns with mental health among their students—with anxiety, depression, and relationship concerns leading the issues being treated—addressing student care in the classroom is becoming increasingly important for instructors across disciplines (APA, 2013).

In chapter 6, Rebecca Hains, who has extensive experience as a public intellectual on the internet and who has published with mainstream media sources like the *Washington Post*, gives practical advice for other instructors and writers on dealing with online harassment. She focuses on how to protect one's mental health, reputation, and jobs when attacks come from the digital public sphere.

Chapter 7 continues the conversation with an administrative perspective on public perceptions of university employees. Administrators must balance the needs of many publics, including alumni, donors, parents, and others, with instructors' needs to do their work and be able to freely express themselves in a public sphere. David Perlmutter moved from the professoriate to become a dean at Texas Tech University. He discusses the balance that administrators must strike between the public and the institution, which can create high levels of stress and strain on university leaders. Perlmutter provides insight into the processes that administrators undergo when making decisions that can affect classrooms and public support, ranging from alumni attendance to donations.

Part II changes the focus to tolerance. Chapter 8 offers practical advice on engaging students in the classroom by "flipping the script." Marquita Smith and Mia Moody-Ramirez outline strategies and exercises using blended learning in the classroom. They recommend the "difficult dialogues" framework to address critical examinations of race, gender, class, sexuality, and other hot-button topics.

In chapter 9, Steve Fox outlines his advocacy for women in the sports journalism classroom after his teaching experiences revealed the sexual harassment many women face. He also gives tips on how to tamp down the "bro culture" that permeates sports journalism.

Student media advisors often are in a tough position when it comes to balancing student journalists' press freedom with administrators' demands. In chapter 10, Meg Heckman addresses pressures on advisors regarding campus sexual abuse and mandatory reporting requirements. Because faculty are mandatory reporters under federal Title IX laws, advisors are being placed in precarious positions when their students report on sexual misconduct, including assault and harassment. Instructors also are being forced to reveal information students give them in confidence. Heckman offers specific advice and resources for instructors and students.

Chapter 11 brings together three leaders from the Native American Journalists Association (NAJA) to discuss approaches to teaching and reporting on Indian country. Victoria LaPoe, Lenzy Krehbiel-Burton, and

Rebecca Landsberry discuss approaches to topics pertinent to Native American communities. These include so-called parachute reporting, stories about Native American mascot representations, Halloween costumes that co-opt Native images and identities, and how to accurately portray communities, with the goal of reducing mediated stereotyping and erasures of Native identities and perspectives. This chapter brings the experience and knowledge of NAJA leaders into conversation with the mainstream media to give professors and students some hands-on, practical advice for classroom exercises and reporting tips for raising awareness of Native American stereotypes.

Did you ever have someone (probably a man) try to explain things to you when you're already an expert in that area? If you've been on the other end of such infuriating condescension, then you will want to read chapter 12 on mansplaining. Laura Castañeda offers class activities to draw attention to and prevent this scourge. You also may want to read this chapter if you want to avoid committing such an offense.

In chapter 13, Khadija Ejaz, a recent graduate of the University of South Carolina, discusses the ways that identity, student perceptions, and instructor authority collide in university classrooms for new graduate student teaching courses. She shares personal reflections and those of other graduate students on teaching difficult topics for the first time, especially as a woman and a person of color.

Chapter 14 focuses on ways to use mediated texts of LGBTQ representations to foster discussions of intersectionality in classrooms. Nathian Rodriguez recommends ways to employ critical pedagogy through various pop culture texts, including videos, podcasts, streaming shows, and music. Rodriguez argues that such an approach can help students question and respond to oppressive ideologies in media and mass communication.

Paromita Pain discusses the importance of intersectionality in the classroom in chapter 15 and suggests ways to create a classroom environment that supports and encourages intersectional conversations. Intersectionality may seem like an intimidating topic at first, so Pain's chapter gives a definition of the term and some commonsense approaches. By breaking it down, Pain makes intersectionality approachable and usable by both students and professors.

In chapter 16, Candi Carter Olson and Tracy Everbach add a final reflection on what diversity means to teaching journalism and mass communication on the college and university level.

The book closes by providing different types of resources for teaching tolerance, including books, videos, films, academic journal articles, popular articles, and interactive online projects. This resource list also offers links to sites that will help you learn more about the topics discussed in this book and gives further tips and tricks for making your classroom a safe and challenging space for approaching tough topics.

Together, these chapters cover many of the issues and ideas that make tough topics challenging for university instructors. This book uses a peer-to-peer approach to addressing these ideas and making them approachable. Avoiding the issues won't make them go away. Tackling them in a thoughtful and creative way can make the experience insightful, useful, and inspiring for students and professors.

REFERENCES

American Psychological Association. (2013). College students' mental health is a growing concern, survey finds. *Monitor on Psychology, 44*(6). Retrieved from https://www.apa.org/monitor/2013/06/college-students.

Cohen, S. (2016, April 11). A brief history of sexual harassment in America before Anita Hill. *Time*. Retrieved from https://time.com/4286575/sexual-harassment-before-anita-hill/.

Covaleskie, J. F. (2019). Speech, academic freedom, and privilege. *AAUP Journal of Academic Freedom, 10*.

Falkoff, M. (2018, April 25). Why we must stop relying on student ratings of teaching. *The Chronicle of Higher Education*. Retrieved from https://www.chronicle.com/article/Why-We-Must-Stop-Relying-on/243213.

Flaherty, C. (2019a, May 20.) Teaching evals: Bias and tenure. *Inside Higher Ed*. Retrieved from https://www.insidehighered.com/news/2019/05/20/fighting-gender-bias-student-evaluations-teaching-and-tenures-effect-instruction.

Flaherty, C. (2019b, September 10). Speaking out against student evals. *Inside Higher Ed*. Retrieved from https://www.insidehighered.com/news/2019/09/10/sociologists-and-more-dozen-other-professional-groups-speak-out-against-student.

Hudson, D. L. (2017). Rights of teachers. *The First Amendment Encyclopedia*. Retrieved from https://www.mtsu.edu/first-amendment/article/973/rights-of-teachers.

Kamola, I. (2019). Dear administrators: To protect your faculty from right-wing attacks, follow the money. *AAUP Journal of Academic Freedom, 10*.

Lawrence, J. W. (2018, May-June). Student evaluations of teaching are not valid. *AAUP*. Retrieved from https://www.aaup.org/article/student-evaluations-teaching-are-not-valid#.XW0kq5NKgUQ.

McClennen, S. A. (2019, September 15). Why are college students so stressed out? It's not because they're "snowflakes." *Salon*. Retrieved from https://www.salon.com/2019/09/15/why-are-college-students-so-stressed-out-its-not-because-theyre-snowflakes/.

Phillips-Fein, K. (2019, January 31). How the right learned to loathe higher education. *ChronicleVitae*. Retrieved from https://www.chronicle.com/article/How-the-Right-Learned-to/245580.

Vasey, C., & Carroll, L. (2016, May-June). How do we evaluate teaching? Findings from a survey of faculty members. AAUP. Retrieved from https://www.aaup .org/article/how-do-we-evaluate-teaching#.WrFBzOgbNPY%0A.

Weale, S. (2019, May 22). Higher education staff suffer "epidemic" of poor mental health. *The Guardian*. Retrieved from https://www.theguardian.com/ education/2019/may/23/higher-education-staff-suffer-epidemic-of-poor -mental-health.

Part I

CONFRONTING
TOUGH TOPICS

2

Walking with Our Students

Turning Theory-based Courses into Hands-on Media Production Opportunities

Candi Carter Olson

"The work you're going to be doing is missionary work." These words, said to me by the man who hired me to teach all of the tough, "don't touch those in class" media literacy topics in Utah, a notoriously conservative state, have guided my hand. Every tough topic—race, class, religion, ethnicity, disability, gender, sexuality, and more—comes up at least once a year in my class. What keeps me going is that student, and there's at least one every term, who comes up to me and says, "Thank you. I identify as [name your identity here; I've had many] and I've never had another teacher talk about these issues in class. I feel seen for the first time in my life." Teaching media literacy, which includes race, class, gender, sexuality, disability, and other issues of social difference, is a very different kind of missionary work, but it still changes lives.

As a professor, I see teaching a theory-based media literacy class such as Gender and the Media as an opportunity to change the statistics and raise a generation of people who are willing to challenge popular narratives that are damaging to survivors of various kinds of identity-based violence and erasures. Access to the media and to equal representation in the media is a privilege that allows a group the power to tell narratives that counter the dominant storyline. As UN Women's 2018 infographic on women and the media notes (see figure 2.1), only 9 percent of news stories currently discuss gender inequality, and only 4 percent of stories challenge gender stereotypes. While women are around 50 percent of the world population, they are only a quarter of the people read about in news stories. Online media has just opened a new realm for abuse of

2 out of every 10 women have been harassed online

1 in 2 women were sent unwanted explicit images

9% of news stories discuss gender inequality; 4% challenge stereotypes

Information from UN Women's "Infographic: Women and the Media"
Designed by Candi Carter Olson

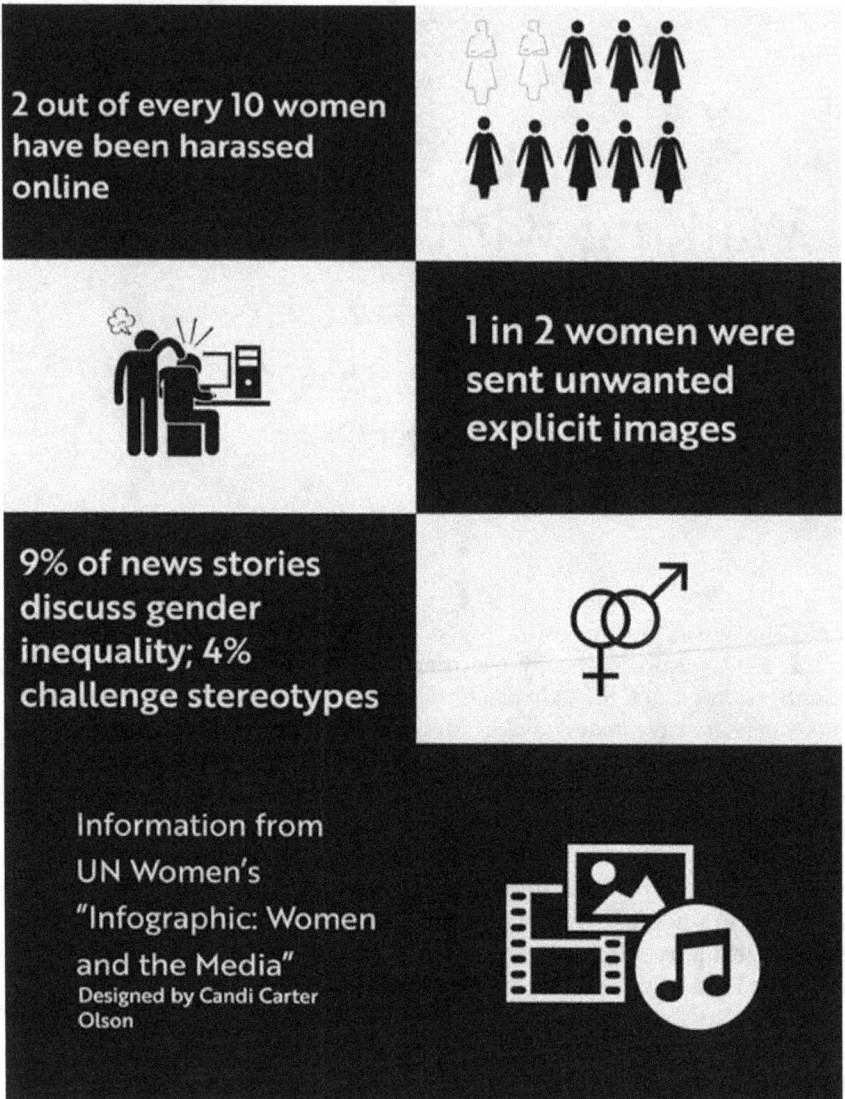

Figure 2.1.   Women and the media. UN Women, 2018.

women, too. In the United States, two of every ten women ages eighteen to twenty-nine say they've been harassed online, and one in two said they were sent unwanted explicit images (UN Women, 2018).

Media literacy classes present an opportunity to train the next generation to challenge these numbers. Media is a powerful tool for putting stories back into the hands of students. Through hands-on media projects, students grasp the enormity of the mediated world confronting them daily. They also feel empowered to tell counternarrative stories that challenge and broaden the conversation in their own communities. Goodman (2018) notes that media literacy conversations are often about "building a more inclusive and humane school culture that will not only benefit the most vulnerable students, but also promote greater empathy and mutual understanding among all students" (p. 83). This chapter focuses on the importance of walking beside our students and giving them the tools to become media literate and empowered media consumers. Paolo Freire's (2000) concept of decentering the professor and empowering the learner undergirds all of the assignments in this chapter.

All of the projects described in this chapter are aimed at individual communities, but the broader goal is to turn out students who are empowered to be media producers changing the broader media environment. To make meaningful change in mediated conversations, we have to start with our own communities. Much of identity-based media production deals with the aesthetics of trauma, particularly in the era of #MeToo when stories about power brokers' and politicians' sexual misconduct are splashed broadly across front pages. Media can turn that trauma into a productive conversation and push out mirrors so that those who have not seen themselves projected in the media previously find their image reflected. The goal is seizing the opportunity presented to us to change patriarchal structures within the academy and outside of it: "Being who we are, doing what we do, enmeshes us (and our students) in contradictions, contradictions potentially generative of change in our educational system, perhaps even in the deepest structures of our gender arrangements" (Culley, et al., 2012, p. 11).

To do this, I've tested my media literacy classes with a variety of assignments that move students from being passive consumers to active producers of diverse media content. These assignments are scaffolded from the least emotional investment to the most potential emotional confrontation. These assignments begin with analyzing the messages in our environment using cell phones and a simple walk around campus. The second takes students through the historical development and reinforcement of a stereotype to produce an encyclopedia-like exploration of the stereotype and its historical distribution through the media. The final assignment challenges students to produce media for a client that runs a counternarrative.

CLASSROOM CHALLENGES

Exercise 1: Diversity Cell Phone Scavenger Hunt

This first exercise is an icebreaker that starts students on a path toward more difficult work later. The purpose of this exercise is to make students

aware of the media they are passively consuming every day and to understand the messages being communicated to us about body image, gender,
sexuality, ability, race, and religion. According to Red Crow Marketing, Inc.,
Americans are exposed to four thousand to ten thousand ads each day,
many of which we passively screen out of our active thought processes to
avoid information overload (Simpson, 2017, para. 3). However, because we
screen to retain our mental sanity and not get overwhelmed, only about
a hundred ads manage to break through our "attention wall" each day
(Marshall, 2015, para. 7). For this exercise, use student cell phones to your
advantage. Most college campuses are either near a busy thoroughfare
filled with restaurants and stores, or they have a student center filled with
ads and posters promoting everything from health and beauty products to
the university. You can use either of these locations for this exercise.

1. 20 minutes. Have your students get up and take a walk. They will
   need to take out their cell phones and take a picture of every single
   ad or poster that features a person. Have them email you all of their
   photos as they are taking them. (Do not have them text the pictures
   unless you have an easy way to transfer pics from your phone to
   a slideshow.)
2. While students are walking, compile all of their photos into a slideshow. The slideshow does not have to be pretty. It just needs to
   feature all of the ads. You will probably take an extra ten minutes of
   class time to finish your slideshow once all of your students return.
3. 30–45 minutes. Go through the slideshow multiple times. Ask students to tally how many women they see versus how many men
   versus how many gender nonbinary people they see. Then ask
   students how many obvious racial or ethnic minorities they see featured in the images. On the third flip through, ask students for age
   ranges for each of the people featured in the ads. On your fourth
   round through, tally the body sizes of people who are featured. Finally, ask students to tally families, couples, and other relationships
   that may show some kind of either hegemony or diversity. On each
   run through the slides, ask students what activities each gender,
   racial and ethnic minority, age, body size, and family or relationship
   grouping is doing.

   You should have a chart showing each of the categories and its
   related profession and/or activity by the end of your 30–45 minutes.
4. 15–20 minutes. Discuss what patterns students see in the data they
   collected on their walk around campus. What do these images tell
   us about who we think is the "perfect" college student, and who is
   appropriate for our campuses? What do these images tell us about
   bodies and the bodies that are acceptable in our spaces? What do
   the images tell us about success and who is considered successful?

Troubleshooting: The biggest issue with this exercise is that students will feed you the same images repeatedly because they are in the same places. If you have a large enough campus, try to send students to different places around campus to gather their information. Also, reinforce to students that we cannot tell a person's racial or ethnic identity in an image unless it's explicitly named. Students will tend to want to put specific labels on people. Finally, as I noted above, don't have students text you images unless you have an easy way to transfer to a slideshow that can be projected in class. Email is much easier for transferring images quickly and easily.

Exercise 2: Stereotyping Encyclopedia Entries

The purpose of this exercise is to get students to understand the history of stereotypes. Gender, sexuality, race, class, and ability stereotypes are all fair game for stereotype explorations, so this exercise can work for a multiplicity of classes that focus on intersectional issues.

Day 1

1. 10–15 minutes. To start, go to the Ferris State University Jim Crow Museum of Racist Memorabilia website (https://www.ferris.edu/jimcrow/). Have students read "Why I Collect Racist Items" under "About Us/Contact/Hours." Discuss with students how stereotypes about a broad range of groups of people are monetized, from women (the entire dieting and makeup industries) to LGBTQ+ people (all of the rainbow items that come out in June) to minority racial and ethnic identities, like those found in the museum.
2. 30–45 minutes. Break students into groups. Under "The Museum," look at the list of racist caricatures. Give each group one of the caricatures. Have the students read through the write up and then present their caricature to the group. What is the stereotype? How has media been an important part of disseminating and replicating the stereotype? How does gender and sexuality work with the racial and ethnic parts of the stereotype to create the full caricature?
3. Any class time that is left. Have students brainstorm as many stereotypes about as many groups as they can and write them on the board. It helps to put group names on the board so that students can start thinking. Men and women work as broad categories, but you may need to add in intersectional identities, such as "Black women" and "Black men" and "Latinx women." Each group needs to choose the stereotype that they would like to work with for the rest of the week. Students may start out feeling uncomfortable naming stereotypes, so be prepared to list a few yourself just to get the ball rolling.

The more specific you are in narrowing categories, the more specific your students will be about identifying the intersectional identities that go into the development of a stereotype. You don't want students to talk about Hawai'ians. You want students to examine the stereotype of the hula girl or the dumb Hawai'ian surfer dude. There is enough information on each specific category to do encyclopedia entries.

Days 2 and 3

1. Reserve a space in the library near your special collections and work with a special collections librarian to have resources pulled for students on particular stereotypes. Archivists and librarians in general are fantastic people, and you should definitely ask to have a research librarian and/or an archivist on hand for your students to consult.
2. In groups, have students create their own encyclopedia entries on a stereotype in the style of the Jim Crow Museum of Racist Memorabilia.
3. Have one student in each group search the archives to find a historic example of your stereotype to start laying a foundation for how long the stereotype has existed and in how many ways the type has been used.
4. Have the rest of the group research (a) the history of the stereotype and how it has been used in Western societies in both positive and negative ways. If students find positives, have them note why the positives may not be as encouraging as we might first think. And (b), find four instances of places where the media has used the stereotype to sell an idea or character. Students can use anything from ads to TV shows to music videos to movies to find their media examples.
5. Have groups create a small website about their stereotype featuring its history and development and the ways that it has been used by the media.
6. Have students post their final multimedia sites on a group discussion board so that the entire class can see everyone's work and comment on it or get ideas for their future work.

Troubleshooting: The biggest glitch you may encounter with this project is that students won't be able to find an archival item to include in their project, or they won't know how to include it well. To help with this problem, I recommend gathering topics from students as they leave class on Day 1 of this project. Then feed those topics to your archivist and ask them to pull items that may be specifically useful for those topics. Also, space out students in the archives over the two days that you're in the library. Don't let everyone rush special collections all at once. If you do a few at a time, librarians will have an easier time working with individual groups and making sure they get what they need.

Exercise 3: Gender-based Violence PSA

The purpose of this exercise is to get students to create mediated products that are countercultural, in some ways, and take gender and sexuality theory and put it to use in practical products that reasonably could be used by a real-world client dealing with gender-based violence. I have used two clients for this project: the Men's Anti-Violence Network of Utah and my own university. Because this project is so sensitive, please note that the troubleshooting part of this project is going to be much longer and deal with some heavy topics.

I'm not giving time periods for this assignment because this one could take several days or just a couple of days, depending on your course demands. Before starting this project, please be sure that your students have access to counseling services and support systems immediately, if they should need it. This is a project where you will need to do constant check-ins with students to make sure everyone is OK and everything is moving along. Detox at the end of class or just do a quick "How is everyone doing?" check-in at the beginning of each class.

1. First, agree on an issue related to gender-based violence that your client would like made into public service announcements (PSAs). I've always done video PSAs, but you could do social media campaigns or a mix of the two.
2. Arrange students into groups. My classes always contain a mix of students familiar with media production and those who have never done media production. I always make sure that my groups are composed of a mix of students from both so that everyone feels like they can contribute.
3. Give a range of readings, including statistics and state laws, on your issue. Be sure to include controversy around #MeToo and examine the ways that discussing sexual assault and harassment can retraumatize some people. Theory should have preceded this project, but you will need to discuss trauma and mediated trauma at some point during this project. The readings should include information that students might use in the mediated product itself.
4. Bring in your client to speak to your students and introduce the topic and the restrictions of the project itself. I've brought in our university's Title IX coordinator, a counselor from the student office for sexual assault interventions, and members of our university's public relations office, when we've worked for the university. These are just some examples of people who may be helpful to use in your classes.

Note that the people you choose should fit your topics. My students have produced anti–domestic violence PSAs aimed at a non-cisgender female audience, PSAs for a university Upstander campaign, and PSAs for a university Start by Believing campaign.

5. Introduce the concept of creating countercultural media products for use and have students brainstorm concepts that are both countercultural and fit the client specifications. In many cases, just producing mediated products on these topics is countercultural because people don't openly talk about gender-based violence, even in the wake of #MeToo.
6. Have students storyboard their campaigns and then peer review them in groups.
7. Once students have produced rough drafts, bring in the client and have the entire class review the projects and give feedback intermixed with client feedback. I always have at least one group that scraps their entire concept and starts from scratch at this point.
8. Turn the final drafts over to the client for use. We've had campaigns placed in our student center and run before basketball games.

Troubleshooting: This is a sensitive topic, so it's important to take a few things into consideration. First, one in five people in the college age group is a survivor. This means that you will have survivors in your class in all likelihood, and you will have survivors viewing the final project. It's important to take this into account, particularly in terms of who you use in your PSAs.

Students use their fellow students in these projects all the time. However, students don't know if one of their fellow students has ever been accused or perhaps has not been accused but has still been a perpetrator and the survivor has been silent for one of many reasons, including self-protection. One year, one of our PSAs that was chosen by our client turned out to have a perpetrator in it and no one knew because the survivor had not reported the incident yet. The video was, understandably, traumatizing for the survivor. We, however, didn't know until this person self-disclosed about the assault and had to report the assault to different people on campus before the PSA could be removed from circulation.

This led our group to agreeing to only use trained student representatives from our sexual violence center in PSAs. This answer won't work for everyone, but if there is a group of trained, safe students on your campus, this is one solution. Another solution is to only use students in student government, since those students are already university representatives. However, being elected to an office does not exempt a student from being a perpetrator. The other solution is to only use class members in the PSAs, as, presumably, students taking a Gender and the Media class would be better informed and less likely to be perpetrators—although I find that survivors tend to take this course in higher numbers—than other students. This assumption could also be wrong, of course, and could lead to issues, as well.

This last part about survivors taking Gender and the Media in higher numbers is anecdotal, but I always have multiple students who self-disclose to me or to the entire class during the process of this project or at some other point during the class. My university, like many academic institutions, has a mandatory reporting requirement. In this instance, the topic is coming up as part of the course material, and the events don't necessarily happen on campus, which puts this in a gray area when it comes to Title IX reporting requirements. In these cases, I have done the following:

1. Asked the student if they had intervention services and offered to walk them to our office of student sexual assault intervention services. I have walked multiple students to this office and made sure they were enrolled in services.
2. Walked students to counseling services, if they did not have a counselor and needed one.
3. Informed students that I am a mandatory reporter and told them that I would pass their name along to Title IX; however, they did not have to respond to anything that Title IX sent, if they were not comfortable doing so. I do inform students, though, that Title IX could help them with classes if they were struggling and arrange a schedule that helps them avoid taking a class with their perpetrator, if that is a problem. I try to be as clear as possible about services students can get from each of the various places that I take them so they know exactly what they need. Sometimes survivors don't know that they need a resource until they find out that it's available and they could benefit from the service.

It's important that we instructors educate ourselves on the various services available to our students both on and off campus. Survivors are sometimes in pure endurance mode and don't have the resilience to research their options themselves. Our job is not to be a counselor. Our job is to connect students to the services that already exist on our campus and make it clear that we are safe, informed people to speak to about anything.

Just teaching these classes makes us a resource. Therefore, it's part of our duty to our students to be informed and willing to talk with students and walk with them as far as they need us to go. Going for help is intimidating, and having someone who is willing to walk with you, even if that person is your professor, is empowering. Always walk with your students. This will make you a strong ally on campus.

Also, remember that secondary survivors—roommates, siblings, and friends of primary assault survivors—are undergoing trauma, as well. They are on the front line of intervening with assault survivors because they're often the first people to whom a survivor will disclose. Secondary survivors will need services just as much as the primary survivor. Be willing to introduce the concept of secondary survivors to your students and note that resources through Title IX and the office of sexual assault services are available to them, as well.

Each of these three exercises raises different conversations and can be used to steer students toward considering the media's role in proliferating gender-based stereotypes. The emotional investment inherent in each varies in vulnerability as they progress, but that emotional vulnerability is necessary for discussing gender topics. Our classes are inherently vulnerable, and they require a teacher who is willing to decenter themselves and walk beside their students rather than leading from in front. As Steven Goodman (2018) writes,

> Program interventions and strong support from teachers and school leaders will go a long way toward building a more inclusive and humane school culture that will not only benefit the most vulnerable students, but also help promote greater empathy and understanding among all students. In some cases, being a compassionate, dependable, and supportive adult may save lives. But in every case, they are helping transform them. (p. 83)

REFERENCES

Culley, M., Diamond, A, Edwards, L., Lennox, S., & Portuges, C. (2012). The politics of nurturance. In M. Culley & C. Portuges (Eds.), *Gendered subjects: The dynamics of feminist teaching*. New York, NY: Routledge.

Friere, P. (2000). *Pedagogy of the oppressed: 30th anniversary edition*. New York, NY: Bloomsbury Academic.

Goodman, S. (2018). *It's not about grit: Trauma, inequity, and the power of transformative teaching*. New York, NY: Teacher's College Press.

Marshall, R. (2015). How many ads do you see in one day? Red Crow Marketing, Inc. Retrieved from https://www.redcrowmarketing.com/2015/09/10/many-ads-see-one-day/.

Simpson, J. (2017). Finding brand success in the digital world. *Forbes*. Retrieved from https://www.forbes.com/sites/forbesagencycouncil/2017/08/25/finding-brand-success-in-the-digital-world/#ecb62a2626e2.

UN Women. (n.d.). Women and the Media: The Beijing platform for action turns 20. Retrieved from http://beijing20.unwomen.org/en/in-focus/media.

UN Women. (2018). Infographic: women and the media. November 23, 2015; updated March 2018. Retrieved from http://www.unwomen.org/en/digital-library/multimedia/2015/11/infographic-women-and-media.

3

Taking Heat

Navigating Diversity and Confrontation in the Classroom

Tracy Everbach

"Homeless people are just lazy and they don't want to get a job," the student said. It was one of the last classes of the semester. Nearly every session the same student, a young white man, had made insensitive comments. A student who sat in the row behind him, a young Black man whose family once was homeless, had had enough. He jumped out of his seat, fists clenched.

"Man, I have been listening to you mouth off all semester, and I can't take it anymore," he said. "I feel like punching you right now."

I walked over to the agitated student, put my hands on his shoulders from behind, and said, "Let's walk outside."

My large, upper-level journalism class, Race, Gender and the Media: A Methods Approach, is a constant learning experience. Conflict and controversy are part of the landscape. No matter how much instructors think we understand about underrepresented groups—race/ethnicity, gender, poverty, sexuality, disability—we're likely to be faced at some point with classroom disputes about these topics.

Through teaching this class for more than a decade, I have encountered many contentious moments. I've also learned lifelong lessons. The most rewarding part is hearing students say the class helped them change their way of thinking about mass media, themselves, and others not like them.

I teach at a large, diverse university, and my classes are populated with students of different ethnicities, religions, sexualities, gender identities, abilities, and economic backgrounds. The diversity creates a powerful educational experience while challenging ingrained ideas. Students react and relate to stories from peers who describe facing bigotry and discrimination or, on the flip side, receiving support and advocacy.

The near-fistfight that day ended on a positive note. I spoke to the agitated student outside the classroom and told him to come back inside when he felt calmer. When he did, the student who had insulted him apologized.

These types of conflicts happen in classes focused on diversity, but they also occur in other classroom settings. Any class in journalism and mass communication will touch on divisive issues like immigration, race/ethnicity, police brutality, sexual abuse and harassment, and/or white supremacy. Controversial topics can be difficult to address in a classroom. My approach is to provide students with intellectual tools to reach conclusions through factual information, ethical considerations, and analysis.

Students also deserve empathy and compassion. In addition, instructors may point out false equivalencies; for example, if a journalist is reporting about the Black Lives Matter movement, it is not necessary to include the positions of the Ku Klux Klan as an "alternative viewpoint." David Gooblar (2019) of the University of Iowa's Rhetoric Department writes, "We're not looking to teach students every possible perspective on an issue is equally true. Rather we need to teach them how to base their conclusions on argument and evidence—even if that evidence conflicts with their prior beliefs" (para. 14).

I offer here some techniques and approaches that have worked in my classroom when confronting emotional topics.

SET GROUND RULES FOR CIVIL DISCUSSIONS

In the syllabus and on the first day of class, I announce my expectations for classroom discussions. The syllabus reads: "Discussion is a major component to this class. Students are encouraged to discuss, debate and dissect the topics we study in a civil and intellectual manner." No name-calling is allowed in class, and if students represent a particular position or opinion, they are expected to back it up with facts.

Lara Schwartz and Daniel Ritter of the Project on Civil Discourse at American University recommend employing a "responsibilities" framework. This type of discourse encourages students, instructors, and administrators to consider the effects of different types of speech on communities, and to use that speech "productively and wisely" (Schwartz & Ritter, 2019). Civil discourse, the authors note, is "truthful, productive, and audience-centered," and it is the responsibility of the instructor to enforce it.

I encourage students to listen to their peers' stories and learn from them. For example, African American students often talk in class about being pulled over by police for no reason, being followed around stores, and being overlooked in classes. In one class, some white students gasped when an African American student described being pulled over by police for no reason while driving a Lincoln SUV. He said the police first asked where he got the vehicle, and when he explained he was a college student and his parents gave it to him, the officers ordered him out and demanded to see his college ID to prove he was a student. Also, many women students have told stories about work colleagues sexually harassing and groping them, enduring catcalls while walking, and being treated as less intelligent than men. LGBTQ students have spoken of rejection and misunderstanding from religious leaders and family members, even being kicked out of their homes for their orientations. Listening to these stories teaches students to have empathy and compassion for their peers.

EMPHASIZE AN ACADEMIC APPROACH

Tell students from day one that this is a class based on research methods and theories, not on opinion. This sets a tone that they are not to debate their beliefs or opinions, but to discuss scholarly research and facts. My predecessors who developed and taught this class, Dr. Meta Carstarphen of the University of Oklahoma and Dr. Jacqueline Lambiase of Texas Christian University, brilliantly added "A Research Approach" to the title "Race, Gender and the Media." They created assignments that would require students to create research projects using qualitative, quantitative, and historical methods, and to apply mass communication theories. These academic skills empower students to conduct their own research and discover their own results. (An example of an assignment appears in a text box on page 26.)

To emphasize that course content is based on established research, I use multiple media, including a textbook, documentaries, popular press articles, scholarly articles, movies, music videos, and online videos, such as TED talks. Theory is part of the curriculum. For example, during each discussion, I ask students how the topic relates to various theoretical concepts, including agenda-setting theory, feminist theory, critical race theory, cultivation theory, social learning theory, symbolic annihilation, hegemony, and more. (A list of suggested class resources appears at the end of this book.)

Guest speakers, experts in their areas, also add to the learning experience. I invite several each semester to discuss their lives and communities. For instance, after a student asked in class, "Aren't Muslim women oppressed?" I invited two Muslim women who wear hijab to speak. One is a former student who is now a writer and the other is a lawyer. They spent forty-five minutes explaining their choice to wear hijab. Several

MEDIA ANALYSIS ASSIGNMENT EXAMPLE

Choice of One

1. **History:** Find an old news magazine, newspaper, film, television series, or advertising campaign that would have been available to one of your elder family members or friends at a designated place and time. This artifact should be at least twenty years old. Discern patterns of depictions of people. Are stereotypes included, either overtly or more subtly? How did you identify these? Why do you think these depictions are used? Are there patterns of these depictions? What about photos, headlines, cutlines, bylines, story placement, table of contents, scenes? Who are the sources quoted? Who are the characters depicted? What do these elements reveal about representations in that era? ALSO: Interview your elder family member or friend to discuss your findings, your assumptions, and conclusions, and see whether these match his or her own perceptions of that era's news media coverage. You'll write a three- to four-page, double-spaced report of your own findings (mini-content analysis), incorporating the comments from your interview with the family member or friend (oral history). Attach a sample of what you analyzed. Can you tie your findings to any of the theories or concepts we have discussed in class? If so, discuss them.

OR

2. **Content Analysis:** Complete a content analysis of news media, entertainment media, or advertising, using the tools of qualitative and/or quantitative research. For example, choose a website, magazine, TV program, film(s), or newspaper. Create a body of texts to study, such as first-page or homepage stories, top stories in newscasts, or sports coverage. Or choose a movie or movies, television shows, roles of particular people in movies or TV shows, an advertising campaign, portrayals of particular people in ads, video games, music videos, or other facets of entertainment media. You should analyze the text for aspects of race, gender, sexuality, or other topics we have discussed in class. You can choose one or more aspects. You'll write a three- to four-page, double-spaced report of your own findings (mini-content analysis), including numbers along with descriptive analysis that helps you find patterns or themes. Attach original charts or graphs of the numbers you counted or themes you found (if you did so) and/or a sample of what you analyzed (e.g., photos or links). Be sure to note what is significant about your findings and point out both positive and negative implications. Can you tie your findings to any of the theories or concepts we have discussed in class? If so, discuss them.

interested students remained after that night class to talk further to the women. Another former student who is Muslim asked me if he could talk to the class about Islamophobia. He returns every semester, and students appreciate hearing from someone who once was in their seats. A speaker who works for an LGBTQ resource center shares his collection of historical media representations of his community. His is always one of the most popular classes of the semester.

ACKNOWLEDGE YOUR OWN PRIVILEGE

One of the first things I tell students is that I'm aware of my unearned advantages because I am a white woman. Yes, I acknowledge, I worked very hard to become a journalist and a professor, but I also received a head start in life simply because I have lighter skin. This shows students of color that I understand the discrimination they have faced and still do on a daily basis. It also signals to white students that they should examine their own advantages. Sociologist Robin D'Angelo in her 2018 bestselling book, *White Fragility: Why It's So Hard for White People to Talk about Racism,* writes about the need for white people in particular to realize that racism is an institutional and systemic problem rather than an individual one.

"White people raised in Western society are conditioned into a white supremacist worldview because it is the bedrock of our society and its institutions," D'Angelo writes. "Regardless of whether a parent told you everyone was equal, or the poster in the hall of your white suburban school proclaimed the value of diversity, or you have traveled abroad, or you have people of color in your workplace or family, the ubiquitous socializing power of white supremacy cannot be avoided" (2018, p. 129).

By "white supremacy," she does not mean neo-Nazis or other hate groups like the ones who marched in Charlottesville, Virginia, in August 2017 during the "Unite the Right" rally. D'Angelo refers to the dominant ideology under which Western society operates, with the assumption that whiteness is the norm. Racism, she argues, is systematic and embedded. "White supremacy in this context does not refer to individual white people and their individual intentions or actions but to an overarching political, economic, and social system of domination" (p. 28).

For instructors, it may help to understand that people progress through different stages before they acknowledge their own racial identity. White students (and faculty) often wrestle with victim-blaming, guilt, and/or idealism before they embrace their racial identities and understand how to become allies to people of color (Fox, 2009). Because of this, white students may need empathy, help, and encouragement. I've repeatedly heard from white male students about how difficult it is to take the class and learn and accept that people who look like them have done harm to women and people of color.

Male instructors of all races are advised to recognize their status as the default gender. Most Western leaders are assumed to be men. You're likely to score points with students by acknowledging that men, unlike women, usually receive respect and are assumed to be in charge. As an example, I have to tell students at the beginning of class how to address me (Dr. Everbach or Professor Everbach) because some male students think it is appropriate to call me "Miss" or "Mrs." Male professors usually receive the courtesy of being addressed with an appropriate title that shows respect and contains no reference to their marital status.

ENSURE A SAFE LEARNING ENVIRONMENT

A few times over the years, students have left my classroom in tears during discussions. Others have asked to be excused from particular discussion topics, such as violence against women. One of the most important jobs of an instructor is ensuring students have a safe learning environment. I sometimes feel I have let them down, even though it's impossible to know every student's individual background or what might cause them grief.

At the beginning of the semester, I tell students that at some point some of the class material or discussions might make them feel uncomfortable, including material relating to rape, sexual assault, and family or partner violence. If they feel overwhelmed, they are allowed to leave the classroom. We hear that one in five college students has been raped or sexually assaulted, but the true number likely is higher. Family and intimate partner violence also is more prevalent than we realize. Talking frankly and openly about these topics, with facts, figures, and statistics, is vital.

At times students have made naive or ignorant comments in class, such as "Why don't women who are abused just leave?" or "Why would anyone want to be transgender?" As an instructor, it is your job to moderate discussions and make sure students who are distressed know they have support and can get help. Talking to them one-on-one to say you care is a way to start. You also can refer them to the college or university counseling center or another office to receive professional support and help. After one particularly emotional discussion about family violence, I asked the Dean of Students' office for backup. They sent their survivor advocate to discuss consent, violence, and other traumatic topics with the class. Afterward, two students apologized for callous remarks they had made.

Some students come to class with the intent of challenging or baiting the instructor. There is nothing wrong with a student asking questions; however, some students will cross the line and disrupt the educational environment. If a student interrupts class or intentionally tries to gain negative attention, it's important to address the problem immediately. Tell the student that he (it's most likely a he) can come to your office to talk about the issue in person, or ask the student to meet with you before or after class. Tell the student he is disrupting your class and you will not tolerate such behavior. Some students are surprised when I talk to them about this because they don't realize what they are doing or they don't want to acknowledge it. Confronting the behavior usually solves the problem.

That said, never tolerate harassment, abuse, or violence. You have every right to tell a student to leave your classroom. One student several years ago became upset after I cut him off for continuing to talk about irrelevant topics. He waited for me after class, outside in the dark (it was a night class), and started yelling that I had "violated his First Amendment rights." After I told him it was my class and he needed to obey the rules, he stormed off. Later I told this story to the university police chief, and he said I should have called the police. I agree. I should have.

Other factors that may influence students' classroom behavior include mental health, family issues, and external social pressures that are causing mental distress. However, these stressors do not excuse poor behavior. Again, you do not have to tolerate disruptive behavior, but finding a workaround helps. I did not understand at the time why the student at the beginning of this chapter was consistently speaking out. I discovered a solution, though: Every time he began to rant, I'd tell him to stop, and we'd talk about it after class. He wasn't very happy about that, but the other students were.

EMPLOY TEAM-BASED LEARNING AND SELF-REFLECTION

Most instructors and students in large classes are familiar with a phenomenon that the same students continuously offer their thoughts and analyses, while the rest of the students remain silent. Also, students tend to sit with and talk with others who are like them. For years, I grappled with how to address this in my classes, until I attended some training sessions on team-based learning. While team-based learning has specific tenets, I decided to adapt a few of its principles for my class. Before each semester starts, I obtain a list of enrolled students and their photos. Although photos do not always reveal students' full backgrounds, they can help in identifying students' ethnicity and gender. On the first day of class I announce groups of five or six, which I work to ensure are diverse in ethnicity and gender. The groups work together and sit together during the semester, present one of the readings, and host a class discussion. This ensures all students have contact with a variety of their peers.

Students also are required to keep an individual blog to write and reflect about their learning. They choose the platform and the name of the blog, sharing the URL with the instructor. (That way they can write anonymously if they don't want to use their name.) These personal blogs remain on the internet so that students can refer back to them and observe their progression from the beginning to the end of the course.

FINAL THOUGHTS

One of the most important tips for teaching a class like this is to keep a sense of humor. Sometimes the topics are heavy and the truth can be depressing, but if you can still use humor along with humility, it creates a feeling of unity. For instance, during the fall semester, right before Thanksgiving break, I tell students, "Have fun discussing everything you have been learning in class with your family when you go home!" Jokes can cut tension and provide relief. I also like to show clips from the comedians Key & Peele's Comedy Central show because they address serious issues about race in a comical way.

Another tip is to share positive stories of people helping others, standing up for others, or being recognized for good work involving diversity. You can ask students to tell the class about some upbeat news that's happened to them. Small gestures can create an optimistic tone.

You may get to a point in class where students feel discouraged from discussing bigotry and inequality. Students have asked, what can we do to solve racism, or misogyny, or homophobia? I reply that of course we can't individually eradicate these ills, but one way to start fighting them is to acknowledge one's own biases. After that, we can actively engage in ways to avoid them. In a class exercise, I ask students to close their eyes, then envision a CEO, a senator, and a professor (or sometimes, a senator, a doctor, and a professor). When they open their eyes, I say, "Chances are, you probably thought of three middle-aged white males. Well guess what, *I'm* a professor, and when I close my eyes I see an older white-haired man in a tweed jacket!" This shows them how ingrained such thought is and how we must fight assumptions every day.

Finally, I'm often asked where we draw the line at offensive comments. How does one determine if something is offensive or "just a joke?" My meter on this is whether it harms another person. Treating everyone like a human being is simple but effective advice.

REFERENCES

D'Angelo, R. (2018). *White fragility: Why it's so hard for white people to talk about racism.* Boston, MA: Beacon Press.

Fox, H. (2009). *When race breaks out: Conversations about race and racism in college classrooms.* New York, NY: Peter Lang Publishing.

Gooblar, D. (2019). What is "indoctrination?" And how do we avoid it in class? *ChronicleVitae.* Retrieved from https://chroniclevitae.com/news/2163-what-is-indoctrination-and-how-do-we-avoid-it-in-class.

Schwartz, L., & Ritter, D. (2019). Civil discourse in the classroom: Simple approaches to tough conversations. American Association of University Professors. Retrieved from https://www.aaup.org/article/civil-discourse-classroom#.XSeHXmRKjZs.

4

Making the Invisible Valuable

Strategies for Translating Work at the Margins

Meredith Clark

Sprawled across my bed, phone in hand, one May night in 2017, I scrolled through real-time photos and videos of young, white, torch-carrying men walking across my new employer's massive lawn and wondered whether I'd made a grave mistake.

When a ragtag band of the Ku Klux Klan traveled to my new hometown of Charlottesville the same weekend I'd planned to move in, I left all of my belongings in two enormous steel lockers outside of my condo and wondered whether it'd be bad form to give up a tenure-track job that more than five hundred people had applied for and live with my partner while I waited for next year's job postings to appear.

But as I drove back into town on August 13 of that same year, I knew that my call to service—planted by my parents' commitment to our faith and nurtured by my education at an HBCU—was about to be tested in ways that defy the academy's triumvirate metrics for tenure and promotion. Being a Black woman hired into a predominantly white institution (PWI), I stepped into a situation Patricia A. Matthew summarized perfectly in a reflection for *The Atlantic* following the 2016 election: "When faculty of color are hired, they are often expected to occupy a certain set of roles: to serve as mentors, inspirations, and guides—to be the racial conscience of their institutions while not ruffling too many of the wrong feathers" (p. 2).

How can we ethically and strategically position our personal commitment to service in ways that satisfies our professional obligations while challenging existing power structures to recognize the often invisible work we do to make our institutions more just, inclusive, and support-ive spaces? Our choice to enter the academy requires us to participate in fundamentally flawed systems, leaving those of us committed to social justice with a daily dilemma: How do we inspire revolution by exploit-ing the institution's systems? And how do we do it in a way that helps us continue to earn a living while creating spaces where people from the margins are served in ways that support their ability to survive and thrive as they pass through? In this chapter, I offer one suggestion for creating an individualized strategic service plan for making the often invisible work of teachers from underrepresented groups visible and valued according to neoliberal institutions where efficiency is praised over all else (Berg & Seeber, 2016; Cannella & Koro-Ljungberg, 2017).

Let me be clear: I write this from the precarious position of being a pre-tenure scholar. It is an exercise of radical imagination, the liminal condi-tion that higher education scholar Shawn Ginwright defines as living in the world that should be, rather than the one that is. As uncomfortable as living and working in this in-between is, as a Black woman in academia, it is the only space I know. I take my cues from the legacy of freedom fight-ers whose work is chronicled in both analog and digital texts, and I pres-ent this chapter as evidence of how their vision and work is being applied in my own life. Having begun my doctoral studies during a political era I never thought I'd live to see—with a White House administration headed by a Black man, Barack Hussein Obama—and finishing them at the height of the movement for Black Lives Matter, I am surrounded by a great cloud of witnesses who decided that the status quo would not stand and took action to implement their vision of what could be. What I desire, in my own time within this space, is for the whole of our invisible labor to first be formally recognized as equally valued within that system, and then to have that recognition work as a catalyst for building systems of liberation and community for all who would pursue the life of the mind (Heinert & Philipps, 2017; Social Sciences Feminist Network, 2017).

In their prescriptive guide to Black academics, Rockquemore and Laszl-offy (2008) confront the paradox of hyper(in)visibility that early career faculty at the margins may face when it comes to service obligations (Gee & Norton, 2009). We are the quintessential faculty called to serve on every diversity committee, task force, and advisory group with a mission that connects to our background, and often, our research interests. Burdened with racial and cultural tax borne of our scarcity in higher education, we are propelled into the roles of ambassador, social worker, oracle, and con-fidant—sometimes all in the same day (Padilla, 1994). For many of us, the commitment to service that goes beyond simply showing up and having our perspectives put on the record in committee meetings and informally advising students who draw into our orbit is one of a joyful (if tired) servant. We realize that our existence on campus is itself a revelatory act—something I'm reminded of every day when I pass the serpentine brick walls that enslaved Black laborers built to cloak and silence their toiling to build "Mr. Jefferson's" precious Academical Village.

This service is isolating and can be costly; it is the result of a special kind of hyper(in)visibility and tokenization that Hirshfield & Joseph (2012) note in their examination of the cultural tax levied at the intersection of race and gender among women of color faculty members in the Midwest. One Black woman in Boice's (2000) research recalled with specificity the wounds created by overcommitment and overreliance to "do the work" of diversity for her institution: "What hurt me most was the time I spent on committees that just had to have a Black and a woman among its members. What killed me was the time and energy that so many, many needy Black students needed from me" (p. 255).

The aggrieved professor recalled how her time was spent performing emotional labor, a concept Arlie Russell Hochschild introduced in her 1979 article, "Emotion Work, Feeling Rules, and Social Structure," to describe the affective efforts that public-facing workers, including flight attendants, call-center employees, and others, do to manage their own emotions as their work demands they prioritize the comfort of the consumer. The term was adopted in digital and social media spaces to describe the translational labor people who are already "navigating the borderlands" of identity and belonging are often expected to do as one of a few (or sometimes the only) person of their background in an otherwise homogenous work or social environment—a condition shared by many minoritized teachers in higher education (Anzaldúza, 2012; Harris & Nicolazzo, 2017).

Quantifying the expense of this time and energy and channeling it into productive outcomes that serve our career progression must be a part of our tactical engagement with the academy's demands. In my purview, this begins with an account of time, one of the few personal, yet shared, nonrenewable resources we each have. Were we members of any other profession, there would be external controls to at least account for the time we spend doing tasks that relate to the general well-being of the university.

Generally speaking, medical doctors work in definitively limited shifts. Hourly wage workers are scheduled and paid to the extent that their employers can afford their time. Lawyers count billable hours in fifteen-minute increments. How many hours did you spend consulting on diversity issues or shadow advising students whose needs are invisible to your institution? How many fifteen-minute lessons have you given well-meaning colleagues who call on you for peer therapy to talk through their discomfort with cultural issues they experienced in the classroom (Bellas, 1999)? How many people have asked to see or use the syllabi you've intentionally crafted to include the perspectives from people of color, people with disabilities, people who are nonbinary, and the host of people typically overlooked as intellectuals in our field? Each of these points of engagement gives critical service to our respective institutions, the field, and the world at large. And the effort behind them demands that they be valued both internally and externally.

One of the ways I approach this is by reflexively writing about these experiences and thinking of ways I can incorporate these notes into my research. I also keep track of the investment of time in a hodge-podge of ways: as entries on my calendar, as columns of figures running in the margins of my calendar. At the end of every month, I have a solid estimate of how much time I've invested doing cultural work that benefits the university and the field; at the end of every year, I have a corpus of autoethnographic field notes that—assuming I have the motivation and time—can inform a conference presentation, a workshop, or even a peer-reviewed journal article on a topic related to my work on race, media, and power. I am confident that we all have this unharvested material in our stores and can use it to make sense of our own research, teaching, and service, while providing insights for our colleagues (Stanley, 2006; Yoon, 2019).

We can move it from inquiry into resistance praxis by using it to meet tenure expectations. Low-investment approaches include quantifying our service hours on our vitae and annual reviews (an expectation we have for the high school students who want to attend college); more demanding is translating this work into talking points, memos, fieldnotes, and ultimately journal articles, book chapters, and other information goods to be assessed as research activity. But consider the radical possibilities: How much of your time could you account for and defend if you had an accurate count at the end of the month? How many articles, supplemental to the scope of your research, could you produce over the course of your career by drawing on those notes each summer to write a literature review about a topic you confronted, or an autoethnography of a cultural issue you experience in your day-to-day work? Such work is timely, possible, and necessary. The volume that you are currently reading is the product of such critical self-reflection about the moral, ethical, and cultural work that this group of journalism and mass communication scholars do to improve the spheres where we live and work.

Knowledge of the university's explicit and inferred needs is essential to quantifying our efforts. In the wake of the affirmative action push of the 1990s, through the corporate citizenship model that is espoused today, most institutions have one or more statements about their commitment to diversity (Kim & Patet, 2018). These provide a framework for making invisible emotional labor measurable and quantifiable by the university's standards. Formally, this includes creating calendar entries that I can search when I sit down to compile my annual review and quantify in terms of time. I also draw connections between my service efforts and student outcomes. For every student who receives a recommendation letter from me and wins an internship, job, or access to a graduate program, I count that as part of my service efforts. While these letters are a small part of the overall consideration, in most cases, they are also integral to the student's selection and should not be discounted by a blanket description of service to the department. How many letters of recommendation have you written in the last year? Do you know how long each one took to draft? You should.

I recommend three strategies for simplifying these efforts on a personal level. First, based on the recommendations of mentors, including Donna Y. Ford and Cathy Mazak, I encourage all faculty members, regardless of rank or status, to write a statement of their guiding principles. Call it a mission statement or an organizational device, but I encourage you to try to do it in no more than 280 characters—a tactic I developed to help my students write their professional elevator pitches for use across platforms. (Bonus points if you can crunch it down to 140.) Memorize it, because you're going to need it when you turn down the myriad opportunities and decline to accept additional obligations that don't fit within its scope. Keep it visible, because you'll need to shift between it and email requests for very worthwhile service efforts that don't fit within its scope. Integrate it into your annual review, and where applicable, your probationary and/or tenure review files, because it will be a key device in your narrative of how your work links the domains evaluated for promotion. My mission statement, if you will, says: "My labor concentrates on the intersections of research, media, and power. I use a mixed-methods approach to explore how these factors influence outcomes for members of underrepresented groups, especially Black women in the United States."

That's it. It's the North Star guiding my decisions about what projects to take and create, and how to make those projects valuable to the institution. Per Mazak's guidance, I learned to consult my mission statement before saying yes to new research projects, and with time, I learned to consider it before agreeing to any obligation of my time.

Reiterating the advice to know what your institution values, as part of my preparation for my annual review, I search for language directly from our mission statement, guiding principles, charter, or other document to craft the narrative of this service work's importance. The goal here is threefold: to create a succinct statement that can be used as part of the annual review, to develop a core narrative that can be adapted for tenure review, and to write boilerplate language that can be excerpted and passed on to colleagues who may seek to nominate you for awards related to your work. All too often, some of the hurdles we encounter in being considered for such prizes is that others don't know what we do or how we do it, and we're too humble to brag on ourselves. Crafting these statements and relying on them as part of the canon of your academic existence can help remove these obstacles.

Here's UVA's mission statement:

> The University of Virginia is a public institution of higher learning guided by a founding vision of discovery, innovation, and development of the full potential of talented students from all walks of life. It serves the Commonwealth of Virginia, the nation, and the world by developing responsible citizen leaders and professionals; advancing, preserving, and disseminating knowledge; and providing world-class patient care.
>
> We are defined by:
>
> • Our enduring commitment to a vibrant and unique residential learning environment marked by the free and collegial exchange of ideas;
> • Our unwavering support of a collaborative, diverse community bound together by distinctive foundational values of honor, integrity, trust, and respect;
> • Our universal dedication to excellence and affordable access (2014).

And here's how I connect my own mission statement with that of the university, and operationalize what I do to fit within its expectations: "In the last quarter of this academic year, I have committed more than forty hours of work to upholding the University's avowed commitment of 'unwavering support of a collaborative, diverse community' by addressing the knowledge gap among students from underrepresented groups making their initial forays into professional life. I have applied my research inside the academy in service to the community, meeting our pledge of 'affordable access' to education by consulting with local community groups about the pursuit of racial equity in news media coverage. And in taking a critical-cultural approach to developing the graduate student handbook for our nascent master's degree program, I endeavor to create a lasting legacy of service to the Commonwealth of Virginia through the development of tools essential in the education of our incoming class of citizen leaders."

Even though it causes some inner conflict, I also track every interaction with students that falls under the guise of mentorship or related service. I began this practice last year as I waited in my office, checking the clock, growing increasingly annoyed as I waited for Trisha, a student who'd missed at least six days of class that semester. She quietly shuffled in, more than ten minutes late for our appointment. A quick glance told me she'd recently had her hair done; her long, pink nails looked salon-fresh, too. As we talked about her hardships this semester, I put myself in a colleague's shoes and saw why another professor might have said her need to make up work was "not my problem." If she had time to get her hair and nails done, why did she struggle with my coursework? But as a Black woman, I understood what I was seeing: not an attempt to exploit the system or a compassionate faculty member, but the evidence of cultural influences that emphasize a demand not to look like what we're going through. Trisha was indeed struggling. That her appearance didn't show it was an intricate ruse to give her some semblance of control in an otherwise overwhelming set of personal circumstances and a defense mechanism against appearing weak or substandard in an academic culture where she was constantly reminded that she is an outsider. We talked for an hour, working through how to balance managing her mother's illness and her final semester. We walked through how to make written and in-person appeals to professors who'd written her off as flaky because she missed classes as she traveled back and forth to her hometown to watch her grammar-school-age siblings while her mother was hospitalized—a familial obligation for which there's no doctor's excuse. We discussed self-care, too, and ways for her to preserve her own mental health as she took the final steps toward becoming the first college graduate in her family. She worked the plan and everything worked out, allowing Trisha to graduate on time when she otherwise might have failed, just a semester shy of finishing college.

While faculty often talk a good game about supporting the complex needs of students from underrepresented groups, I've sat in a number of faculty meetings, committee meetings, and one-to-one conversations where its clear privilege blinds colleagues to what that actually means. Admittedly, it can be difficult to recognize what students need beyond the steps they require. Time is one of their most critical needs, and our investment of time, emotional labor, and cultural labor should be included in our assessment of how we go about doing our jobs. Each year, our promotion and tenure reviews ask us to quantify our research, teaching, and service efforts. The first two are arguably easier to do than the third, especially when that service is the invisible work of informally counseling students on the margins, providing a sympathetic ear or advice; helping them strategize to work past the invisible obstacles of privilege, including assumed cultural knowledge. But we can quantify this work and present it as labor with significant value to the university, our departments, and the profession.

One way is to engage in a bit of autoethnographic content analysis. Assuming you keep a calendar, I encourage you to pull it out and highlight every instance of service-related work connected to your mission statement. Examples from my own schedule include the informal counseling I gave my student Trisha and the handful of students who ask to meet with me simply because I'm the first Black professor they've ever had; consulting with a local human resources commission on questions they should ask the city's newspaper staff about how they cover Black communities; advising two students on attending a professional conference—from pitching their internship directors for financial support to learning how to identify which workshops and events are worthwhile; and developing our department's graduate student handbook, including an intentional focus on issues of diversity and inclusion. All told, these add up to more than forty hours of service that remains true to my own personal and professional goals. Identifying how this work dovetails with the institution's mission at both the departmental and university levels and writing about those connections can bring them into focus.

I assume an assimilationist-activist approach to this work, recognizing that we must be in the proverbial room, at the metaphorical table, in order to make these changes. Yet whether we sit in the folding chair we brought along for the journey or in a seat of leadership, I believe that these strategies, collectively practiced, shared, proven, and reinforced at every level and within multiple institutions, can be a useful tool for helping faculty reflexively find the commodified value in our service in a way that does not force us to equivocate about our personal mission of working for social justice in neoliberal institutions.

REFERENCES

Anzaldúza, G. (2012). *Borderlands/La Frontera: The new Metiza*. San Francisco, CA: Aunt Lute Books.

Bellas, M. (1999). Emotional labor in academia: The case of professors. *The Annals of the American Academy of Political and Social Science, 561*, 96–110. Retrieved from http://www.jstor.org/stable/1049284.

Berg, M., & Seeber, B. K. (2016). *The slow professor: Challenging the culture of speed in the academy*. Toronto: University of Toronto Press.

Boice, R. (2000). *Advice for new faculty members*. Needham Heights, MA: Allyn and Bacon.

Cannella, G. S., & Koro-Ljungberg, M. (2017). Neoliberalism in higher education: Can we understand? Can we resist and survive? Can we become without neoliberalism? *Cultural Studies ↔ Critical Methodologies, 17*(3), 155–162. Retrieved from https://journals.sagepub.com/doi/abs/10.1177/1532708617706117?journalCode=csca.

Gee, M. V., & Norton, S. M. (2009). Improving the status of women in the academy. *Thought & Action, 26*, 163–170.

Harris, J. C., & Nicolazzo, Z. (2017). Navigating the academic borderlands as multiracial and trans* faculty members. *Critical Studies in Education*. DOI: 10.1080/17508487.2017.1356340.

Heinert, J., & Philipps, C. (2017). From feminized to feminist labor: Strategies for creating feminist working conditions. In K. Cole and H. Hassel (Eds.), *Composi-*

tion, in surviving sexism in academia: Strategies for feminist leadership (127–135). New York, NY: Routledge.

Hirshfield, L. E., & Joseph, T. D. (2012). "We need a woman, we need a Black woman": Gender, race, and identity taxation in the academy, *Gender and Education*, 24(2), 213–227. DOI: 10.1080/09540253.2011.606208.

Hochschild, A. R. (1979). Emotion work, feeling rules, and social structure. *The American Journal of Sociology, 85*(3), 551–575.

Kim, K., & Patet, P. (2018). The (Im)possibility of (Un)doing diversity in teacher education: (In)visibility of faculty of color in the accreditation standards. *Race Ethnicity and Education.* DOI: 10.1080/13613324.2018.1511526.

Matthew, P. (2016). What is faculty diversity worth to a university? *The Atlantic.* Retrieved July 19, 2019, from https://www.theatlantic.com/education/archive/2016/11/what-is-faculty-diversity-worth-to-a-university/508334/.

Padilla, A. (1994). Ethnic minority scholars, research and mentoring: Current and future issues. *Educational Researcher, 23*(4), 24–27.

Rockquemore, K. A., & Laszloffy, T. (2008). *The Black academic's guide to winning tenure without losing your soul.* Boulder: Lynne Rienner Publishing.

Social Sciences Feminist Network Research Interest Group. (2017). The burden of invisible work in academia: Social inequalities and time use in five university departments. *Humboldt Journal of Social Relations, 39*, 228–245. Retrieved from http://www.jstor.org/stable/90007882.

Stanley, C. A. (2006). Coloring the academic landscape: Faculty of color breaking the silence in predominantly white colleges and universities. *American Educational Research Journal, 43*(4), 701–736. https://doi.org/10.3102/00028312043004701.

University Code of Ethics and Mission Statement. 2014. The University of Virginia. Retrieved from https://www.virginia.edu/statementofpurpose.

Yoon, I. H. (2019). Hauntings of a Korean American woman researcher in the field. *International Journal of Qualitative Studies in Education, 32*(5), 447–464. DOI: 10.1080/09518398.2019.159721.

5

Pedagogy of the Stressed

Mental Health in the Mass Communication Classroom and on Campuses

Chelsea Reynolds

Rachel[1] texted me at midnight. "Professor, I'm in the emergency room, and I missed tonight's story deadline," she wrote. "I had a panic attack and suicidal thoughts, so I called an ambulance. What can I do to make up my points?"

Weeks later, my iPhone buzzed during a faculty meeting, alerting me to Maria's message on Twitter. "My mother lost her battle with cancer," she typed. "I don't know if I will be able to complete my reporting portfolio before the end of finals week, so I'm asking for an extension."

Fast-forward a few short months. "This may come as a shock," a stranger's voice trembled on my office line. "I got your name from Daniel's syllabus. They found him unresponsive last week. We're looking for answers."

Each semester, journalism and mass communication faculty members field countless emails and meeting requests that illuminate our students' struggles with mental health, grief, and addiction. Data collected in 2018 by the American College Health Association show that more than half of U.S. college students reported feeling hopeless and nearly 40 percent had experienced debilitating depression within the past twelve months (American College Health Association, 2018). A National Survey of College Counseling Centers survey found that 94 percent of university counselors reported spikes in student reports of severe psychological issues, such as sexual assault trauma and self-harm (Gallagher, 2015).

---

1. Students' names have been changed to retain anonymity.

Everyday stressors on students are compounded by the pressures of our field—a tumultuous 24/7 news cycle and a contentious political climate for media professionals.

We must conceptualize mental health as a public health crisis in mass communication classrooms and on college campuses. As faculty members, our ethical duty is to provide compassionate learning environments that teach emotional accountability and transparency. Faculty must be prepared to not only respond to requests from undergraduate and graduate students who reach out for help, but we must develop forward-thinking curricula that approach emotional intelligence head-on. Pedagogical theorists such as Janice Marie Collins at the University of Illinois Department of Journalism have argued that mass communication educators should share the goal of "making the inside and outside of the classroom, and the world in general, a kinder, safer, more equitable place to thrive" (Collins, 2019). As faculty, we must also be ready to cope with the emotional demands placed on us as teachers and advisors. Expectations for emotional labor are compounded for faculty who are women, people of color, or members of the LGBTQ community (El-Alayli, Hansen-Brown, & Ceynar, 2018; Schueths et al., 2013).

This chapter offers resources for instructors who hope to introduce emotional intelligence and mental health as learning outcomes in their courses—both for themselves and their students. In the following pages, I provide pedagogical interventions that will help instructors improve their classrooms' psychological wellness. My interventions include a flex absence policy, a stress assessment tool, a sleep contract, and a self-care activity.

MENTAL HEALTH ON CAMPUS

College students face immense emotional pressure and are often traumatized or retraumatized during their first year on campus (Galatzer-Levy, Burton, & Bonanno, 2012). Those traumas can be acute, as when my student Kari was sexually assaulted at a frat party. Trauma can also accrue over time, as with my student Jordan, who spent their entire childhood navigating a tumultuous foster care system. Trauma can even be passed on from generation to generation or from members of a student's community (Brave Heart, Chase, Elkins, & Altschul, 2011). At the California State University system, where I teach, more than one in ten students has faced homelessness and 40 percent of students face food insecurity, though those rates are alarmingly higher among African American students (Crutchfield & Maguire, 2019). Across the United States, 11 percent of students are single parents (Kruvelis, Cruse, & Gault, 2017). More than

40 percent of undergraduates and 70 percent of graduate students hold a full-time job (Carnevale, Smith, Melton, & Price, 2015). Nearly one in four is coping with alcoholism or drug addiction (Califano, 2007). University enrollees are exhausted, overworked, and unprepared to cope with the financial and psychological stressors associated with campus life.

More than half of all students surveyed by the American College Health Association (ACHA) reported feeling hopeless during the last year, and roughly 85 percent reported feeling overwhelmed by all they have to do (ACHA, 2018). Many, like my student Anika, doubt their ability to perform in a high-stress media work environment when they experience social anxiety or depression. Mental illness among student populations is similar to that of the general population, and women report being diagnosed with mental illness at more than double the rate of their male peers (ACHA, 2018). According to the National Alliance on Mental Illness (NAMI; 2019), one in five Americans is living with a mental illness, and twice as many women reported self-harming in the past thirty days than did men. One in twelve students had actively made a suicide plan (ACHA, 2018).

Like other variables measured by surveys of college life, mental illness is more prevalent among student groups that face multiple social pressures. Mental illness is intersectional. Indigenous communities have the highest rates of mental illness diagnoses among racial and ethnic groups at 28.3 percent, while Asian Americans experience the lowest rates of mental illness at 13.9 percent (NAMI, 2019). At my university, students are concerned about their immigration and documentation status, a palpable stress when my reporting classes discuss our country's crisis on the southern border. Further, LGBTQ Americans are twice as likely as the general population to experience mental illness, and LGBTQ youth are two to three times more likely to take their own lives (NAMI, 2019). College-aged women are at three to four times the risk for sexual assault than are women in the general population, with one in five undergraduates experiencing rape or sexual assault before graduation (RAINN, 2019). We must teach our students to think critically about the systemic factors that influence not just physical and mental health, but access to health care as well.

MENTAL HEALTH AND MASS COMMUNICATION

Students enrolled in mass communication programs may face additional pressures that impact their mental health. Our undergraduate majors are committed to extracurricular involvement with student media and professional internships. Once they enter the field, they are expected to work long hours with tight deadlines on low salaries, often launching their careers in small media markets hours away from their hometowns. While negative mental health outcomes are well documented among reporters and news photographers, strategic communication students also need to know that they are not alone if they experience burnout or emotional exhaustion.

That said, young journalists are especially susceptible to burnout, substance abuse, and post-traumatic stress disorder (PTSD), and they are likely to experience a traumatizing event early in their careers (Amend, Kay, & Reilly, 2012; MacDonald, Saliba, Hodgins, & Ovington, 2016; Maxson, 2000). According to a systematic review of literature conducted by the Dart Center, 80 to 100 percent of journalists eventually experience work-related trauma (Smith, Newman, Drevo, & Slaughter, 2019). In a meta-analysis of twenty-eight journal articles published about occupational stressors and their impact on journalists' mental and physical health, the authors found that the most common sources of journalists' stress include job role demands, interpersonal issues in the workplace (including reportorial ethics), physical demands such as noisy newsrooms with low light, work conditions of long hours and low pay, and task-related stressors such as covering high-stress situations and traumatic events (Monteiro, Marques, Pinto, & Roberto, 2016). The same study found that journalists experienced osteo-muscular disorders, burnout, depression, anxiety, PTSD, alcohol and substance use, and job turnover as a result of work-related stress (Monteiro, Marques, Pinto, & Roberto, 2016). More recently, a 2019 survey of 254 newspaper journalists found that covering traumatic events led to "emotional drain, painful flashbacks, anxiety, depression, guilt and coping mechanisms employed, including crying and substance use, such as drinking alcohol" (Seely, 2019). Whether we are training young reporters or strategic communication professionals, our fields' emotional demands may far exceed that of other white-collar professions.

MENTAL WELLNESS AS A CLASSROOM INTERVENTION

By decentralizing our pedagogies from the detached, Western, masculinist style of teaching, we can foster emotional intelligence among the next generation of media professionals, who will in turn contribute to more balanced work cultures in newsrooms and strategic communication firms after graduation. Emotional intelligence can be defined as "an ability to validly reason with emotions and to use emotions to enhance thought" based on an individual's ability to "accurately perceive emotions in oneself and others, use emotions to facilitate thinking, understand emotional meanings, and manage emotions" (Mayer, 2004, p. 3–4).

According to Mayer (2004), people with high emotional intelligence are "particularly good at establishing positive social relationships with others, and avoiding conflicts, fights, and other social altercations. They're particularly good at understanding psychologically healthy living and avoiding such problems as drugs and drug abuse" (p. 8). This makes them sought-after colleagues and employees. Students who prioritize emotional intelligence may be more likely to become leaders in their industries (Mills, 2009). Thus, an investment in student mental health is an investment in the future of media.

In my classrooms, I use feminist pedagogy to invite discussions about uncomfortable topics in the field and in life. Feminist pedagogy assumes a set of expectations, classroom practices, and learning outcomes that envision students and teachers as subjects, not objects, and which creates "a community of learners (that) is empowered to act responsibly toward one another and the subject matter and to apply that learning to social action" (Shrewsbury, 1987, p. 8). On the first day of class, while outlining other pedagogical approaches such as attendance expectations and technology use in the classroom, I introduce a concept called "radical openness"—an approach I have developed in order to foster discussions about the realities of life as a reporter or strategic communicator. "Radical openness" means being transparent about the pressures of a field that often demands more from its workers than it gives back. It also requires being transparent about my own struggles with anxiety, sexual assault, and insomnia, and about my identity as a queer woman. By humanizing myself for my students on the first day of class, learners understand that we are in this together; that professor and student is an arbitrary divide established by the hegemonic logics of the academy, an institution that has historically ensured the subjugation of students under the top-down authority of the (white, straight, male) professor; that learning is a collaborative process; and that emotional intelligence is a key component of a healthy career and a healthy personal life.

SYLLABI AND CAMPUS RESOURCES

Your syllabus should be your first—but absolutely not last—pedagogical intervention for mental health. Prominently list resources your students can use to improve their emotional well-being. Every syllabus you distribute should include phone numbers and hyperlinks for your campus's counseling services office, student disabilities office, LGBTQ resource center, women's center, race and ethnicity offices, university health center, basic needs resources, and immigration consultation center (if applicable). At my university in suburban Los Angeles, our students experience more homelessness, food insecurity, transportation issues, and immigration problems than do students at similar large, public universities across the country. Check with your administrators and talk with your students to better understand the different resources available for folks experiencing financial, intellectual, or emotional duress. Urge your students to review the services available to them on campus.

PEDAGOGICAL INTERVENTION

I developed four standardized mental health interventions that I have adopted in my classrooms. Each of the interventions focuses on building students' responsibility for, transparency about, and accountability toward their mental health. The interventions—flex absences, a stress assessment, a sleep contract, and a self-care reporting exercise—can be adopted sequentially, or they can be used on an as-needed basis depending on your course expectations. The interventions are flexible enough to incorporate within journalism or strategic communications classrooms at the undergraduate and graduate levels. They have the secondary responsibility of improving students' trust in their instructors by fostering an open dialogue about a controversial, often shameful topic. Feel free to tailor my materials to your own classrooms, but please cite the originals in this chapter in your syllabi if you do so.

Flex Absences

A classroom will foster mental well-being only if learners are able to prioritize their emotions. For this reason, it is crucial that emotionally intelligent classrooms integrate significantly more flexibility than might be found in a traditional mass communication curriculum. When I was a graduate student, I leaned on a classroom-as-newsroom pedagogy when developing my syllabi because my instructors at the Missouri School of Journalism had used that model with me. That meant no missed deadlines, no unexcused absences, no bullshit. For a long time I thought the classroom-as-newsroom model meant that my teaching platform had to mirror my editors' demeanor at high-circulation consumer magazines. How else would students learn? I toyed with that question until I realized most of my editors were assholes. Now I try to teach my skills courses as if I were the *best* editor I ever had: I remain attentive and conscientious, rigorous but flexible.

The primary tools I use to encourage emotional accountability are flex absences. I allow students two flex absences (for a twice-a-week, sixteen-week course), in which the students will be excused from class time if they notify me in advance and complete any required course activities on their own time. This provides a low-stakes opportunity for students to skip class if they are feeling anxious, stressed, depressed, or otherwise ill-equipped for attending class. I write the flex absences into my syllabus using the following language:

> Flex absences: I understand that life gets in the way. We have jobs, families, and outside responsibilities. You are permitted two flex absences for the semester, which you can use to tend to these things with no questions asked. You can make up points for the day if you email me about your flex absence by 10 a.m. before class. If you do not email me, you will not be counted as excused from class and you will not have the opportunity to make up points for that day.

Stress Assessment

The first pedagogical intervention is an anonymous survey instrument I call the Stress Assessment (see page 50). It is a simple ten-point scale with accompanying qualitative responses. The quantitative portion asks students to respond to two prompts: (1) Please rate your current stress level in general (1–10, with 1 being low and 10 being high); and (2) Please rate your current stress level related to this class (1–10). The two qualitative questions are (1) What can I do as an instructor to ease your stress? And (2) What can you do as a learner to ease your stress? The Stress Assessment helps identify tensions during high-anxiety parts of the semester, including after syllabus delivery, in the weeks before midterms, and in the weeks ahead of final exams.

The purpose of the stress assessment is to make the students feel supported and heard in the learning environment. Learning is a collaborative process, and certainly mass communication careers demand cooperation and trust among editors and writers, managers and producers, salespeople and creatives, and so on. Much like an employee satisfaction survey would measure workforce morale, I make every attempt to measure the level of pressure my students feel with relation to my courses and their personal lives. After students submit their stress assessments, I analyze students' quantitative stress levels and code the qualitative data according to their themes. Perhaps the average quantitative score for course-related stress is a 7 after syllabus delivery, but students' general stress levels are closer to a 3. If that's the case, my class material is too arduous, and I might consider changing a major deadline or augmenting an existing rubric. If multiple students respond to the qualitative portions that I could ease their stress levels by providing more detail about a specific concept, or by giving examples of a certain reporting strategy, then I build that into the course design.

STRESS ASSESSMENT

DO NOT PUT YOUR NAME ON THIS ASSESSMENT

Please rate your current stress level in general

1	2	3	4	5	6	7	8	9	10
low					medium				high

Please rate your current stress level related to this class

1	2	3	4	5	6	7	8	9	10
low					medium				high

What can I do as an instructor to ease your stress level?

What can you do as a learner to ease your own stress?

Contact information for mental health resources at CAPS: 657-278-3040.

The stress assessment is an informal course evaluation that prioritizes students' humanity in the classroom. Although it provides outlets for students to express their reservations about course material or my teaching style, it also requires that they hold themselves accountable to their stress by considering how they can be better learners. Often students have epiphanies around their sleep or study habits in response to the final qualitative question, identifying self-sabotaging behaviors they can modify to improve their course performance.

Sleep Contract

Sleep makes us functional learners and workers. Sleep hygiene affects everything from memory to decision making, from problem solving to emotional intelligence (Eliasson, Eliasson, & Lettieri, 2017). Sleep habits are a crucial learning outcome for a course designed around mental health. Students often skimp on sleep because they feel pressure to socialize or study late at night, to the detriment of their academic and professional performance (2017). To encourage healthy sleep hygiene, I dedicate some

---

SLEEP CONTRACT

I, _____, certify that I have read the NIH Guide to Healthy Sleep (https://www.nhlbi.nih.gov/files/docs/public/sleep/healthy_sleep.pdf), focusing specifically on pages 19 to 29—"How Much Sleep Is Enough" and "What Disrupts Sleep?"

In exchange for five points extra credit, I commit to sleeping _____ hours per night through finals week, based on my personal sleep needs.

I will be in bed by _____ p.m. I will not use electronic devices with blue screens for at least thirty minutes before I plan to sleep.

_____
Signature

It is your duty to hang on to this slip through finals week. I suggest you post it on your refrigerator or place it somewhere else within eyeshot. At the end of the semester, you can return this slip to me to earn five extra credit points.

This extra credit opportunity is based on the honor system. If you do not attempt in earnest to improve your sleep hygiene, please do not submit the sleep contract.

time at the beginning of the term to administer a sleep contract (see page 51), with an accompanying required reading: *Your Guide to Healthy Sleep* (National Institutes of Health, 2005).

During a thirty-minute in-class activity, I ask students to read pages 19 to 29 of the NIH guide, focusing on the sections "How Much Sleep Is Enough?" and "What Disrupts Sleep?" Afterward, we discuss the importance of rest in high-stress fields such as journalism, advertising, and public relations. The students can elect to sign the sleep contract for five extra credit points. In exchange for five points extra credit, students commit to sleep a set number of hours per night through finals week based on their personal sleep needs, as outlined in the NIH Guide to Healthy Sleep. Students write their bedtime goal on the contract and agree not to use electronic devices with blue screens for at least thirty minutes before bed. After they sign the contract, I log their participation and return the contract sheet to them. I tell my students to hold on to the contract through finals week, displaying it prominently on their refrigerator or on a bulletin board at home. I check in on the students' sleep hygiene throughout the semester by fostering group discussions and reminding them of their contracts. At the end of the semester, students may submit their sleep contracts for extra credit if they give me their word that they earnestly attempted to correct any unhealthy sleep habits. About two-thirds of the students submit the contracts, and another one-third admit that their work, academic life, or social life prevented them from establishing healthy sleep habits.

Self-Care Activity

The most important mental health tool I implement in my classrooms comes at midterm. This is the self-care activity that asks students to take time away from school to focus specifically on an activity that improves their psychological well-being (see page 53). I cancel our class period for the day the self-care activity is assigned. The students are to use class time to complete an activity that benefits their emotional health, such as exercising, meditating, napping, doing creative work, tending to spiritual health, spending time with family or friends, or making a home-cooked meal. Students are not allowed to do school work or homework, consume drugs or alcohol, fool around on social media, drive on Southern California freeways, or do anything else that might jeopardize their ability to take time and space for themselves. Students are to spend ninety minutes on a self-care activity, then report back with a 200-word summary of what they did for self-care, including one picture as evidence. You can tailor this activity to different classes based on the course skills and learning outcomes. For ethics classes, I ask students to reflect about how self-care

COMM 310—MASS MEDIA ETHICS

SELF-CARE ACTIVITY

Today, class will be cancelled. In lieu of our in-person meeting, you are required to do **at least ninety minutes of self-care**. Being an ethical media practitioner means knowing how to take time off and prioritize mental and physical well-being so you can be sharp and logical when ethics issues come up.

Report back with a 200-word summary of what you did for self-care, including one picture as evidence of the self-care you did. **Deadline is 11:59 p.m. tonight.** Include a descriptive title. Write in first person, for example, "This weekend I spent five hours hiking in Malibu with friends, then shared a picnic together on the beach."

Reflect on how caring for yourself can help you care for your work, your colleagues, your peers, and those in your personal life. How will caring for yourself help your ethical decision making at work and at home?

Self-care includes: Going on a walk, taking a swim, napping, making art, eating a good meal, cleaning your house, hitting the gym, reading a leisure book, watching a movie, playing with animals, spending time with family, getting a massage, and so on.

Self-care does not include: Homework or jobs, drinking or drugs, social media, reading news, getting on SoCal freeways.

COMM 201—WRITING & REPORTING THE NEWS

SELF-CARE STORY

Today, class will be canceled. In lieu of our in-person meeting, you are required to do **at least ninety minutes of self-care**. Being a successful journalist means knowing how to take time off and prioritize mental and physical well-being. Our field has a lot of intense emotional demands. You will be a better reporter in the future if you develop healthy coping strategies in college.

You will write a 200-word summary story of what you did for self-care, with one picture. **Deadline is 11:59 p.m. Saturday.** Please include a hed, dek, byline, lede, and story. Write in third-person, for example, "CSUF assistant professor Chelsea Reynolds spent two hours in her rooftop hot tub Monday afternoon." Your self-care story should be structured in inverted pyramid style, with the most important information at the top of the lede. Include the five Ws (who, what, when, where, why, and how) in your lede.

Self-care includes: Going on a walk, taking a swim, napping, making art, eating a good meal, cleaning your house, hitting the gym, reading a leisure book, watching a movie, playing with animals, getting a massage, and so on.

Self-care does not include: Homework or jobs, drinking or drugs, social media, reading news, getting on SoCal freeways.

can help them make better ethical decisions in the workplace (see the "Self-Care Activity" on p. 53); for journalism classes, I ask students to report out a 200-word news story about their self-care activity using third-person voice (see the "Self-Care Story" on p. 53). After the students submit their self-care activity for grading, it is crucial that you host another in-class discussion about the importance of mental health and work–life balance. I typically ask students to do a think-pair-share activity reflecting on what they learned by doing self-care activities, the professional benefits of taking time off, and how they can best implement self-care as part of their regular weekly schedule.

PRACTICING WHAT WE PREACH

My course evaluations have consistently reflected the utility of implementing flex absences, stress assessments, sleep contracts, and self-care activities. Students say my curricula's focus on mental health makes them feel more prepared to tackle the course material. However, all this emphasis on emotional intelligence and psychological processing can sometimes be taxing for you as an instructor. Students may interpret the course structure as an invitation to vent about their personal issues during class time or office hours. In order to ameliorate a potential deluge of student crises, I suggest implementing a policy that limits office hour visits to ten minutes. Your syllabus should outline your office hour policies: any student can stop by to talk about anything related to the course (or otherwise related to their well-being), and you will meet them with open ears. But after ten minutes, their time with you expires, unless you, as an instructor, have identified a pressing academic concern that you can work together to mediate. Otherwise, you send the student with resources for contacting your student wellness center, psychological services, or other resource centers relevant to their success. Setting boundaries is crucial to any effective mental health–focused pedagogy and is part of your personal self-care practice as a mass communication professor.

It is your duty as the instructor to model healthy behavior for your students. I try to be accountable and transparent regarding my own mental health while retaining an air of authority in the classroom. For example, last summer I had a breast cancer scare that interfered with my ability to teach. Rather than avoid the topic or cancel class without explanation, I emailed my summer school students explaining my health background and the test results I was agonizing over. This provided an entry point through which to discuss anxiety, insomnia, and grieving, as my mother lost her battle with breast cancer when I was a young graduate student. My students opened up to me about their personal struggles and provided words of encouragement that, frankly, got me through a few rough days.

I recommend that you practice what you preach with regard to mental health. In each course I teach, I allow myself a flex absence, fill out the stress assessments and sleep contract, and complete a self-care activity when I assign it to my students. I also take at least one day a week away from research and class prep in order to tend to my personal affairs. Other folks I know choose not to answer emails over the weekend, not to work after 8 p.m. any day of the week, or not to respond to work-related messages over holidays and summer vacation. Emotionally intelligent faculty members will demonstrate the benefits of their own pedagogy; they will be more attentive, supportive, and productive instructors and advisors. In turn, their students will be better learners who understand time and stress management, practice flexibility with their future colleagues, and exhibit empathy as a core ethic in their workplace. An added benefit: student course evaluations will sing your praises. Since implementing radical openness and emotional intelligence as part of my pedagogy, my RateMy-Professor page has become saturated with comments such as "honestly one of the best and most caring professors I've ever had" and "you can tell she really cares about her students and tries her best to prepare us for the comm field." By emphasizing emotional accountability and transparency, you can improve not just the quality of your students' work, but the quality of their lives and yours as well.

REFERENCES

Amend, E., Kay, L., & Reilly, R. C. (2012). Journalism on the spot: Ethical dilemmas when covering trauma and the implications for journalism education. *Journal of Mass Media Ethics, 27*(4), 235–247. https://doi.org/10.1080/08900523.2012.74 6113.

American College Health Association (ACHA). (2018). Reference group executive summary: Fall 2018. Retrieved from https://www.acha.org/documents/ncha/ NCHA-II_Fall_2018_Reference_Group_Executive_Summary.pdf.

Brave Heart, M. Y. H., Chase, J., Elkins, J., & Altschul, D. B. (2011). Historical trauma among Indigenous peoples of the Americas: Concepts, research, and clinical considerations. *Journal of Psychoactive Drugs, 43*(4), 282–290.

Califano, J. (2007). Wasting the best and brightest: Alcohol and drug abuse on college campuses. Center on Addiction. Retrieved from https://www.centeronad diction.org/newsroom/op-eds/wasting-best-and-brightest-alcohol-and-drug -abuse-college-campuses.

Carnevale, A. P., Smith, N., Melton, M., & Price, E. (2015). *Learning while earning: The new normal.* Georgetown University Center on Education and the Workforce. Retrieved from https://1gyhoq479ufd3yna29x7ubjn-wpengine.netdna -ssl.com/wp-content/uploads/Working-Learners-Report.pdf.

Collins, J. M. (2019). Janice Marie Collins, Dr.; University of Illinois experts. Retrieved from https://experts.illinois.edu/en/persons/janice-marie-collins.

Crutchfield, R., & Maguire, J. (2019). Study of student service access and basic needs. The California State University. Retrieved from https://www2.calstate .edu/impact-of-the-csu/student-success/basic-needs-initiative/Documents/ BasicNeedsStudy_Phase_3.pdf.

El-Alayli, A., Hansen-Brown, A. A., & Ceynar, M. (2018). Dancing backwards in high heels: Female professors experience more work demands and special favor requests, particularly from academically entitled students. *Sex Roles, 79*(3–4), 136–150. https://doi.org/10.1007/s11199-017-0872-6.

Eliasson, A. H., Eliasson, A. H., & Lettieri, C. J. (2017). Differences in sleep habits, study time, and academic performance between US-born and foreign-born college students. *Sleep and Breathing, 21*(2), 529–533. https://doi.org/10.1007/ s11325-016-1412-2.

Galatzer-Levy, I. R., Burton, C. L., & Bonanno, G. A. (2012). Coping flexibility, potentially traumatic life events, and resilience: A prospective study of college student adjustment. *Journal of Social and Clinical Psychology, 31*(6), 542–567. https://doi.org/10.1521/jscp.2012.31.6.542.

Gallagher, R. P. (2015). National Survey of College Counseling Centers 2014: Project report. The International Association of Counseling Services (IACS). Retrieved from http://d-scholarship.pitt.edu/28178/1/survey_2014.pdf.

Kruvelis, M., Cruse, L. R., & Gault, B. (2017). Single mothers in college: Growing enrollment, financial challenges, and the benefits of attainment. Briefing Paper #C460, Institute for Women's Policy Research. Retrieved from https:// iwpr.org/wp-content/uploads/2017/09/C460_Single-Mothers-Briefing-Pa per-8.21.17-final.pdf.

MacDonald, J. B., Saliba, A. J., Hodgins, G., & Ovington, L. A. (2016). Burnout in journalists: A systematic literature review. *Burnout Research, 3*(2), 34–44. https:// doi.org/10.1016/j.burn.2016.03.001.

Maxson, J. (2000). Training journalism students to deal with trauma: Observing reporters behave like "creeps." *Journalism & Mass Communication Educator, 55*(1), 79–86.

Mayer, J. (2004). What is emotional intelligence? University of New Hampshire Personality Lab. Retrieved from https://scholars.unh.edu/personality_lab/8.

Mills, L. B. (2009). A meta-analysis of the relationship between emotional intelligence and effective leadership. *Journal of Curriculum and Instruction, 3*(2), 22.

Monteiro, S., Marques Pinto, A., & Roberto, M. S. (2016). Job demands, coping, and impacts of occupational stress among journalists: A systematic review. *European Journal of Work and Organizational Psychology, 25*(5), 751–772. https://doi .org/10.1080/1359432X.2015.1114470.

National Alliance on Mental Illness. (2019). Mental health by the numbers. NAMI. Retrieved from https://www.nami.org/Learn-More/Mental-Health-By-the -Numbers.

National Institutes of Health. (2005). *Your guide to healthy sleep*. U.S. Department of Health and Human Services. Retrieved from https://www.nhlbi.nih.gov/files/docs/public/sleep/healthy_sleep.pdf.

Rape, Abuse & Incest National Network (RAINN). (2019). Campus sexual violence: Statistics. Retrieved from https://www.rainn.org/statistics/campus-sexual-violence.

Schueths, A. M., Gladney, T., Crawford, D. M., Bass, K. L., & Moore, H. A. (2013). Passionate pedagogy and emotional labor: Students' responses to learning diversity from diverse instructors. *International Journal of Qualitative Studies in Education, 26*(10), 1259–1276. https://doi.org/10.1080/09518398.2012.731532.

Seely, N. (2019). Journalists and mental health: The psychological toll of covering everyday trauma. *Newspaper Research Journal* 40(2). https://doi.org/10.1177/0739532919835612.

Shrewsbury, C. M. (1987). What is feminist pedagogy? *Women's Studies Quarterly, 15*(3/4), 6–14.

Smith, R., Newman, E., Drevo, S., & Slaughter, A. (2019, update). Covering trauma: Impact on journalists. Dart Center for Journalism & Trauma. Retrieved from http://dartcenter.org/content/covering-trauma-impact-on-journalists.

6

Being a Female Public Intellectual in the Age of Social Media

Navigating Backlash, Mansplainers, and Trolls

Rebecca C. Hains

Before the rise of social media, a relatively small number of professors could be considered public intellectuals. But through their appearances in the mainstream media—particularly elite opinion spaces—public intellectuals shared their work and ideas with mass audiences, helping to shape public opinion.

Today, thanks to changes in the media industries, audiences are more accessible (albeit more fragmented) than in decades past. With the media landscape no longer characterized by one-way communication dominated by four or five major television networks and a newspaper or two of record, we twenty-first-century scholars have a multiplicity of opportunities to engage with the public. The new technologies that help us share our work have a downside, however, as we are now much more accessible to the public than were twentieth-century public intellectuals. We are easy targets for online abuse.

Reflecting broader trends in online harassment, female scholars are more likely to experience serious online harassment than their white, male peers. According to the organization Working to Halt Online Abuse (n.d.), in an eleven-year period, 72.5 percent of those reporting online harassment were women (p. 1). The abuse is gendered and can also be racialized. The situation has become so dire that Amnesty International (2018) published an eight-chapter report documenting the scale of violence and abuse experienced by women on Twitter. The report concluded with a chapter outlining a range of proposed structural solutions, such as more transparency from Twitter about the levels of violence and abuse on their platform; improved reporting mechanisms; more clarity about their interpretation of violence and abuse and how they handle reports; and user education regarding privacy and security features (para. 2). The report also calls on states to address the problem—for example, by creating legislation aligned with international human rights laws that would criminalize the online abuse of and violence against women (para. 31), and by training law enforcement on the harms of online abuse and violence (para. 32).

In the meantime, given the dearth of structural supports and solutions for gendered online abuse, it's crucial for women who are public intellectuals to know how to handle backlash outside our classrooms, within the mediated world. In this chapter, I draw upon my personal experiences as a public intellectual, interviews with three experts in this area, and various other sources to share resources for navigating the often-treacherous, troll-filled waters that await women who become public intellectuals.

BECOMING A PUBLIC INTELLECTUAL: CONSIDERATIONS

In today's media environment, there are many ways to become a public intellectual. Posting on YouTube, Instagram, Twitter, or in a personal blog; hosting a Facebook author page and/or community; writing op-ed pieces; appearing on podcasts; participating in TEDx opportunities; and pitching journalists and producers are all possibilities. Deciding how to best participate in the mediated public sphere is a matter of trial and error. Experiment to figure out where there's an audience for your work and what media mix will best reach them.

Sarah J. Jackson has noticed, however, a double standard on who is expected to be a public intellectual in today's social media environment. Jackson, a presidential associate professor at the Annenberg School for Communication at the University of Pennsylvania, explains:

> People studying media effects don't have to prove their work matters by being online and responding to people's tweets. Being a public intellectual is seen as more legitimate, and more necessary, when you do identity work or social change work. If you study race and social movements, it's assumed that you will be online tweeting about #BlackLivesMatter—even though doing so may invite significant time and labor spent handling online abuse. (personal communication, August 30, 2019)

Furthermore, Jackson notes, public intellectual work may not directly benefit your career. She advises considering whether it would (a) be valued or (b) lead to opportunities of value in your personnel actions. "Ask yourself what will really get you tenure or promotion," Jackson

HOW I BECAME A PUBLIC INTELLECTUAL

After the publication of my first book, *Growing Up With Girl Power: Girl-hood On Screen and in Everyday Life* (2012), I created a website and blog to establish a platform as a children's media culture expert. I began by developing a list of ten topics I could easily blog about—some of which are among my earliest blog posts at RebeccaHains.com. Simultaneously, I noticed posts going viral on Facebook that related to my interests. Whenever I could offer insights on a viral post, I stayed up after my kids fell asleep—or got up before they awoke—to try to be the first blogger to respond. Then, I promoted the heck out of that post.

The formula worked. To offer one example: a group called FCKH8 created a viral video featuring little girls dressed as princesses who shouted, "What the fuck? I'm not some pretty fuckin' helpless princess in distress. I'm pretty fuckin' powerful and ready for success. So what is more offensive? A little girl saying 'fuck,' or the fucking unequal and sexist way society treats girls and women?" The video had shock value, and because of my expertise in princess culture, people kept tagging me on it. People kept discussing it using the frame FCKH8 had introduced—debating whether the video or sexism was more offensive—and wanted my take.

I quickly responded with a blog post titled "FCKH8's 'F-Bomb Princess' Video Isn't Offensive—It's Exploitative," sharing my main point with a Facebook-ready headline, and explained:

> In all the conversation about whether the video is offensive, we need to also consider the ad from a media-literate perspective and consider FCKH8's corporate interests. Was it *right* for FCKH8 to script a slew of swear words into an advertisement featuring young children?
>
> If we follow the money and consider FCKH8's motivations in producing "F-Bombs for Feminism," it's pretty clear that FCKH8 is in the wrong. Although the video purports to be "for [a] good cause"—presumably, to raise awareness of sexism—what they're really promoting is their T-shirts. By putting FCKH8's bottom line ahead of girls' best interests, FCKH8 is being exploitative.

Once I publicized my post on social media, it went viral alongside the video, helping shape the conversation.

My blog is filled with more examples of this type of quick response to a viral post. In each case, I spent at least as much time promoting the blog post as I spent penning it. By monitoring Wordpress's analytic tools, I developed a sense of which strategies were most effective. The outcome: from 2012 to 2016, I published about 125 blog posts, collectively receiving more than 2 million views from more than 1.5 million visitors. Their visibility led to media interviews, a syndication agreement with the *Christian Science Monitor*, and invitations to write op-eds for major newspapers. This platform served as a valuable asset in securing an agent and a contract for my crossover nonfiction book, *The Princess Problem*, which in turn led to even more media coverage, including a double-segment on *The Meredith Vieira Show* and interviews on princess culture in outlets such as the *New York Times*, NPR, and the BBC.

THE VALUE OF OP-EDS

Sarah J. Jackson of the Annenberg School suggests that regardless of what other tactics you may employ, learning to pitch op-eds is crucial. There is "a lot of benefit in placing an op-ed in a really visible place that translates to both academic and mainstream audiences," she explains, and recommends training from the Op-Ed Project to learn how to pitch editors and how to translate your academic work.

"Institutions can host training sessions by the Op-Ed Project," Jackson notes, "to help faculty members place their scholarship in the public sphere. Faculty development offices often have money for such purposes, so check whether your university will bring trainers to campus."

says. "In considering whether it matters to your institution, think about who will be evaluating you. The PR people at the university may value your work as a public intellectual, but at the end of the day, they aren't voting on your tenure."

If you decide being a public intellectual is worthwhile, at the outset you should clarify your goals. Are you looking to publicize a recent book? Raise your national profile before applying for tenure or promotion? Build a platform, post-tenure, to pursue a book contract with a mainstream publisher (which worked for me, as described in "How I Became a Public Intellectual"—see box on p. 61)? As Jennifer Pozner, a media critic and journalist who authored *Reality Bites Back: The Troubling Truth about Guilty Pleasure TV*, explains, "Knowing your goals matters. It will guide you in deciding which outlets are worth giving your time to" (personal communication, August 29, 2019).

WHEN SCHOLARLY EXPERTISE LURES MISOGYNISTS, RACISTS, AND TROLLS

Unfortunately, the greater your visibility, the more trolls you'll lure—especially as a woman. While some will be generic trolls who enjoy disrupting others for fun (or "for the lulz"), others may campaign against you, hoping to see you fired from your job. (For example, see "From the Trenches" on p. 63.) Others will lash out with gendered and/or racialized threats or harassing remarks or images, sometimes targeting others in your network. For instance, Pozner once had to endure a Twitter troll who made an account with the username @JennPoznerFan. He used a gang bang gif for his profile picture. "That's the one I remember most," she says. "Journalists, academics, colleagues, random young women who followed me, were all targeted. . . . I reported and blocked him."

TAKE BACK THE TECH

For a wealth of advice on handling online abuse, particularly gender-based violence, visit the page "Know More" on Take Back the Tech website. There you will find detailed information on extortion, cyberstalking, hate speech, self-care, and how to help friends and colleagues who are being attacked online (https://www.takebackthetech.net/know-more).

Karla Mantilla (2015) has argued that women are uniquely subject to what she calls "gendertrolling," which is "exponentially more vicious, virulent, aggressive, threatening, pervasive, and enduring than generic trolling" (p. 11). Unlike generic trolls, gendertrolls may be well-connected in online sub communities (such as men's rights activist groups, commonly called MRAs), where they whip up mobs that can become "devoted to targeting the designated person" (p. 11).

As Take Back the Tech (2015) has observed, gendertrolls "seem to have a lot of time on their hands, a lot of anger towards women and very little respect for anyone else's right to express themselves freely and without harassment" (para. 3). These abusers' shared goal "is to intimidate and, ultimately, to silence female commentators"—particularly those they have decided have too much influence. When this happens, they make sustained efforts to "silence or discredit" a target and may dox, stalk, or swat her. Doxxing is maliciously publishing a person's private information online, such as home address; and swatting is a form of criminal harassment that uses 911 or a similar emergency service to falsely report a serious emergency, like a bomb threat or murder at the target's home (Quadling, 2015). Doxxing, then, facilitates both stalking and swatting.

Online harassment can interfere with a target's personal and professional life. This phenomenon is so well-known to journalists, activists, and other prominent women that it "discourages women from writing and earning a living online, [and] interferes with their professional lives," as Danielle Keats Citron, a Boston University Law School professor with an expertise in cyber harassment and online abuse, explained in an interview with Karla Mantilla (2015). "It brands them as incompetent workers and inferior sexual objects" (p. 204).

Gendertrolling can also have mental health consequences and cost women time and money. "No matter how hard we attempt to ignore it, this type of gendered harassment—and the sheer volume of it—has severe implications for women's status on the Internet," as Amanda Hess (2017) has recounted.

Threats of rape, death, and stalking can overpower our emotional bandwidth, take up our time, and cost us money through legal fees, online protection

FROM THE TRENCHES

Lori Day is an educational psychologist and consultant and author of the book *Her Next Chapter: How Mother-Daughter Book Clubs Can Help Girls Navigate Malicious Media, Risky Relationships, Girl Gossip, and So Much More.* In 2016, she wrote a satirical piece for *Feminist Current* called "We Need a Mandemic." Playing on the word "pandemic," and very much in the vein of Jonathan Swift's "A Modest Proposal," Day suggested a "mandemic" might solve many man-made problems plaguing our world.

Unfortunately, men's rights activists (MRAs) chose to ignore the piece's satirical nature. After organizing on sites like Reddit and 4chan, MRAs hacked her website, filled her Facebook business page with fake one-star reviews, and inundated her accrediting organization with complaints.

"In the forums, they were encouraging one another, saying things like, 'We need to let parents know not to hire Lori Day,'" she recalls, "because she shouldn't be within 100 feet of boys! She hates men." Then, someone asked, "How should we let her accreditation organization know that she should lose her license and be unable to work with boys?" They began a campaign against her in hopes that she would lose her livelihood.

Day let the organization know what was happening and went dark online. "I took down my professional website and business page so that people couldn't hack it," she recalls. "I had to take everything down for three or four days at a time, and then see if it was safe yet. If I returned and they started again, I'd take it down for a few more days. Finally, after about three weeks, it blew over—but I know I lost potential clients and money."

Meanwhile, Day saw an online forum member publish her home address. Another responded that he lived near her town and would go case her house and report back to the group. She noticed cars driving slowly past her home. They were watching her.

She filed a police report but hadn't realized the officer wouldn't immediately understand. "I thought cops would be aware of the way online harassment against women can become physical violence," she explains, "but I had to explain everything to the beat cop who came to my door: what MRAs are, what swatting is."

She advises preparing for the police being untrained in this area. Be ready to outline exactly what you need. "I had to lay it out for him: that I wanted him to make a note in my record that if the police department receives a call about domestic violence or a robbery at my address, it may actually be a swatting attempt, so to please take these threats against me into account in their response."

services, and missed wages. I've spent countless hours over the past four years logging the online activity of one particularly committed cyberstalker, just in case (para. 12).

Despite this depressing catalogue of the types of problems women face on social media, you may still feel the professional benefits of becoming a public intellectual outweigh the disadvantages. If this is the case, please take a few precautions:

1. **Lock down your personal details on social media.** Trolls who know your hometown and birthdate can use that information to cause all manner of trouble. So keep personal information off of publicly visible sections of your social media profiles and websites. Make sure your publicly searchable online resumes and vitae don't contain your home address or phone number, either.
2. **Opt out of personal broker directories.** Personal broker directories (like Spokeo and Whitepages) publish people's personal details, including birthdate, home address, phone number, family members' names (and their contact information). Search for your name on these sites and request an immediate removal of your personal data through each site's opt-out page. Most sites will remove the information instantly.
3. **Do regular privacy checks** as maintenance on your social media. For example, on Facebook, view your page "as public" and make sure that neither your timeline nor your friends list (which can be used against you by trolls seeking your personal information), or the groups and pages you "like" (where you can be tracked down), are visible.
4. **Make sure your passwords are secure.** Use two-step authentication wherever you can—email, social media accounts, and so on. Also, check whether your cell phone carrier requires a pin to change your account details. (It should.)

Once you've taken those precautions, what can you do if you are, indeed, harassed?

1. **Don't respond.** Trolls are looking for a reaction. If you choose not to respond, you're ruining their fun. They'll move on sooner than they would otherwise.
2. **Don't click any links.** Trolls may send malicious links in an effort to hack your accounts. This includes your campus email. Do *not* click any links or open attachments (they may lead to malware) or reply to the sender.
3. **Change your passwords.** Get ahead of the hackers by changing your passwords with a secure password manager (such as Dashlane, Keeper, or Lastpass).

4. **Document and report.** Take immediate screenshots of any harass-ment and save them to a dedicated folder. Also report harassment to the platform on which it occurs. If it is on your work email, forward to your university's IT security department and to campus police.

5. **Moderate and block trolls at will.** If harassment occurs on a forum you control, like your Facebook page or blog, report and delete the comments, then block the harassers' accounts. You are not obliged to provide strangers with a platform to harass, intimidate, or terror-ize you or anybody else. Your page or site, your rules.

6. **Alert the authorities**, both at school and in your town, if you re-ceive any threats. Even if you have locked down your personal details online, a particularly resourceful and vengeful party may have doxxed you. Make sure campus and local police are informed, in case your harasser files a false police report (aka swatting) that would set the authorities after you.

7. **Investigate and monitor the source of the trolls.** Are you being mobbed? Search for different combinations of your name and your topic/recent headline/relevant terms online and check the results for posts discussing your work. Then, check the comments to see if people are organizing attacks against you. Then, repeat these searches but add names of forums like "Reddit" or "4chan" as search terms, and read whatever threads you find. If you find discussion inciting violence or harassment against you, document the links, take screenshots, and report to the authorities, per number 6 above. Moni-tor these threads and watch for new ones until the fury has subsided.

8. **Seek the support of social media–savvy friends.** They're good moral support, and some may have pseudonymous accounts from which they can occasionally rebut or call out the trolls, keeping you out of the fray. Also, to avoid reading most of the abusive vitriol, consider asking a trusted friend to investigate and monitor, as de-scribed in number 7, on your behalf, bringing to you only the items you must see—those that warrant reports to the authorities.

9. **Let your university PR team know.** Trolls may flood your univer-sity's social media accounts, email accounts, and phone lines with harassment directly or indirectly about you. Be sure the head of public relations knows so that the PR team is prepared to respond and manage institutional social media accounts as needed.

10. **Tell your dean, too.** If a harassment campaign is under way, "Get out ahead of it and tell your dean what's going on," advises Lori Day, an educational psychologist, counselor, and author with exten-sive experience in academia. "Tell your story first, before someone who wants to harm you tells an incomplete story or takes excerpts out of context" (personal communication, August 30, 2019).

11. **Be aware that some media requests for comment are themselves forms of abuse.** Anytime you receive a request for comment or interview—especially in response to a publication or another interview that has generated controversy—research those requests. Find the social media profiles of the would-be interviewer and their media outlet. Is it a partisan site, program, or publication likely to set you up and deliberately attempt to damage your reputation? Skip it.

Does this sound time-consuming? Yes, it is. Does dealing with this kind of abuse constitute another form of invisible labor disproportionately impacting women? Yes, that too. So be sure to document this work. Any time you include a personal narrative in a tenure or promotion dossier, describe

TIPS FOR ENGAGING WITH THE MEDIA

In the event that your social media work or op-ed leads to interview requests, learning to speak to reporters is crucial preparation.

Focus on your main points. I recommend going into any interview—especially one that will be part of a video or audio broadcast—with two or three main points you would like to get across.

Be prepared to pivot. If you're asked a question that is off topic or, frankly, off the wall (as has been my experience on shows like *Fox and Friends*), don't answer it. Instead, pivot: "That's a great question, but what *really* matters is . . ." and turn the conversation back to the points that matter most.

Clarify how you should be credited. Be certain journalists know how you would like to be referenced. I generally spell out that it would be helpful to me professionally if they could refer to me as both a professor at my university *and* as the author of my most recent book.

Radio, video, podcast? Mention your publications. When being interviewed for a broadcast of any length, be sure to reference your own publications at least twice: once toward the beginning of the segment, and once toward the end. For example, I might say, "As I explained in my book *The Princess Problem* . . ." or "As I mentioned in my recent article in [*Journal X*] . . ." to ensure listeners hear about my work.

Does the show that invited you on the air mistreat guests? Don't chance it. "Back when I was a guest on the Bill O'Reilly show," Jennifer Pozner recalls, "he hadn't yet reached the level of arrogance and control that made him semi-regularly turn off the microphone on guests who started to win debates." But by about 2005, Pozner observed that O'Reilly had become invested in making sure that people with opinions that countered his could not possibly be heard. "So, in early/mid-2000s, I started cautioning attendees at my media trainings: 'There is zero reason why you should do that show.' Don't validate the existence of shows that wish to harm you. No matter how well you prepare, you and your research will not get a good shake."

the additional time and invisible labor your media appearances and op-ed writing entail. Your evaluators won't know if you don't tell them.

Finally, when in doubt about what to do, always consider your options through this lens: "If this were a screenshot, would it hurt me?" Ultimately, as public intellectuals, the world is our classroom, and even when the worst trolls are slinging mud at us from behind false screen names, *we* are being judged for our professionalism and composure. So respond as you would in the classroom, or—better still—don't respond at all.

REFERENCES

Amnesty International. (2018). *Toxic Twitter: A toxic place for women.* Retrieved from https://www.amnesty.org/en/latest/research/2018/03/online-violence -against-women-chapter-1/.

Dahlgren, P. (2013). From public to civic intellectuals via online cultures. *Participations: Journal of Audience and Reception Studies, 10*(1), 400–404.

Hains, R. C. (2012). *Growing up with girl power: Girlhood on screen and in everyday life.* New York: Peter Lang.

Hess, A. (2017, June 14). Why some aren't welcome on the internet. *Pacific Standard.* Retrieved from https://psmag.com/social-justice/women-arent -welcome-internet-72170.

Mantilla, K. (2015). *Gendertrolling: How misogyny went viral.* Santa Barbara, CA: Praeger.

Quadling, A. (2015, April 21). Doxxing, swatting and the new trends in online harassment. *The Conversation.* Retrieved from https://theconversation.com/ doxxing-swatting-and-the-new-trends-in-online-harassment-40234.

Take Back the Tech. (2015, Nov. 27). How to take back the tech when trolls appear. Retrieved from https://www.takebackthetech.net/take-action/2015-11-27.

Working to Halt Online Abuse. (n.d.). HaltAbuse.org. Comparison statistics 2000–2011. Retrieved from http://www.haltabuse.org/resources/stats/Cumu lative2000-2011.pdf.

7

A Communication Unit Administrator's Perspective on Speech Controversies in the Classroom and on Campus

David D. Perlmutter

I can pinpoint the worst day of my now-more-than-a-decade of academic administration across three campuses and serving in several roles (associate dean, director, dean). It was the finale of the most challenging week of my professional life as an administrator. On a beautiful Friday afternoon, a walk through downtown, right next to my then-campus (at the University of Iowa), felt like a scene from a dark comedy movie tinctured in pathos accompanied by the Benny Hill soundtrack. Every conversation I heard was about the situation our school faced and I was dealing with in emails, phone calls, personal visits, news articles, and social media each day. Passersby, people waiting at bus stops, diners at the outdoor area of a café—all were talking about us, and none favorably. The theater of the absurd was capped off when I spotted a novelty shop selling T-shirts that referred to our "scandal."

What happened? One of our faculty had written an essay for a prestigious online venue that many state residents—including my relatives by marriage—had interpreted as derogatory about the state and its people. It was, for me personally, a very unhappy period. But it was also a learning opportunity about the modern "campus speech controversy."

We live in an era when both faculty and students may share, post, tweet, forward, or upload content that is the subject of dispute not only in a classroom but elsewhere: on Facebook, Twitter, the front page of the local newspaper, or a CNN newscast (Perlmutter, 2006, 2008, 2018). It is perfectly proper to focus, as most of this book does, on the effects of a controversy on the student and the teacher, but it's important to be aware that other players—those who believe (or unwillingly find) themselves stakeholders—can get involved, including chairs, deans, and beyond in the campus leadership.

I know. I have been there more than once. At one end of the spectrum, students (and parents) have complained to me by phone, email, or in person that a professor has said or done something objectionable. In almost all such cases, administrators can deal with the issues "locally." Perhaps a simple conversation clarifies and appeases; alternatively, some institutional, state, or federal trigger may be engaged (as in a Title IX complaint) that must be handed to other parties.

At the other end of the notoriety scale, I have found myself in a media storm where it seemed like the whole world was upset with what a faculty member in our program said. Yes, in this case the comments were not uttered in the classroom but offered in an online publication, but really—what are the borders of the classroom today? Other cases abound nationally of something said in a classroom that has been uploaded into the public sphere of outrage.

Crucially, though, when a professor tweets or publishes something that gets negative attention, people will still treat it as if the distasteful content impacts the lives and ideologies of students. In other words, speech uttered outside the classroom will be linked to the discussion about what is allowable *inside* the classroom—as in, "Is this the kind of crap you are teaching our kids?" On the other hand, in this era of the smartphone and social media, what a professor says in the "privacy" of the classroom or the office may very well be shared or posted, leading to public outrage. There is simply no expectation that any controversy of speech will be localized anymore. It affects all of us, not just individual faculty or students.

Of course, campus administrators—whether a department chair or the president—should never expect anyone to feel sorry for them. My intention here is not to solicit sympathy for me as a person or for us as a class but rather to

- Offer a perspective on campus controversies other than those of the regular faculty or students.
- Highlight that the effects of a "difficult dialogue" controversy can ripple (or explode) beyond the original actors.
- Review challenges administrators face and tasks we often need to take on when a controversy lands on our desk (as a parent's complaint to us) or spills out into the public sphere (a Twitter storm or angry alumna/us call).
- Demonstrate that there is no single administrative point of view on free speech controversies in academia but only varying kinds of stances and attitudes that administrators have historically taken.

These are often driven by their disciplinary background, which is most likely not journalism and mass communication (hereafter, JMC) or their role (e.g., dean of students, university council).

- Affirm that definitions of academic freedom vary, and even the courts have never specified what such a concept means (Cain, 2018; Di Domenico, 1995; Gruber, 1972; Huq, 2010; Nugent & Flood, 2014).
- Offer a short list of best practices that administrators can consider in response to future campus controversies.

I draw upon controversies I have experienced, witnessed, interviewed other administrators about, and read about in popular and scholarly literature. Indeed, I have been writing about higher education issues and careers in a monthly column for the *Chronicle of Higher Education* for almost twenty years. I also have written a book about promotion and tenure (Perlmutter, 2010).

THE "JOURNALISM ETHIC" IS A MINORITY VOICE ON CAMPUS

Let me begin with a bit of political context: I am a journalism professor. I have never believed that this status conflicted with my administrative titles, but when a campus speech controversy erupts, it can seem like the duties of administration don't always align with the ideals of journalism education.

Second, and perhaps more important, only a small number of campus administrators come from a journalism background. I can count on one hand the number of provosts or presidents I have heard of who once were media and communications faculty. You are far more likely to meet a provost or a president whose academic background involved teaching forestry, industrial engineering, or finance than media ethics or opinion writing. Likewise, many JMC programs are situated in colleges of arts and sciences, where again the dean is much more likely to be a chemistry professor than to originate in journalism. There are more members of governing boards who may have once been a publisher or a chief communications officer at an auto company, but still the overall number of "us" among the higher powers on campus is small or nonexistent.

Why am I emphasizing this? No college administrator is an island. You serve at the pleasure of somebody else and it's likely that the somebody else who is your "boss" doesn't come from the same ideological, ethical, or experiential background you do. We are a minority in our traditions and codes, and once you walk outside (literally and figuratively) the confines of the communications program offices, you know it.

WHAT CAUSES CONTROVERSY AND WHO IS A STAKEHOLDER?

In this section I use the term "campus speech controversy" in a broad and loose sense that will encompass many kinds of events or happenings. Some have more in common than others, and not all instances can fit into one neat category. But for purposes of discussion, campus speech controversy can include

- A faculty member and a student getting into a dispute in the classroom that goes public and gets wider attention on campus and beyond.
- A faculty member sharing, posting, tweeting, or publishing a controversial statement that attracts news industry and public (internet, social media, etc.) notoriety.
- Students protesting by various forms (including social media) some aspect of your program including the conduct or utterances of a faculty member.

Note that in free speech controversies, there always seems to be a mixture of intentionality and naivete. Sometimes you get a feeling that a faculty member who tweeted something provocative intended to poke ideological enemies. At other times, especially in the case of classroom exchanges that go viral, the faculty member is shocked that something that was supposed to be a private interaction within the confines of the educational process has become a public controversy. The outcomes, however, are the same, and they are worth discussing in detail.

Further, I want to put aside how the free speech controversy affects the actual parties involved since other chapters in this book will address this issue. Most administrators prioritize the welfare of colleagues and student charges, but our job is also to be concerned about wider issues that include the following:

1. How will this affect the brand of our university or our program?
2. How will this affect enrollment, and thus, unit revenue?
3. How will this affect fundraising and general donor support now and in the future? (McDonald, 2005; Perlmutter, 2014).
4. How will this affect faculty morale and classroom culture in the future?
5. How will this affect my job—will it get me fired?

All of these concerns can be legitimate and serious and affect what we say and how we react.

Part of the problem is that the narratives one hears and reads about when there is a speech controversy on campus tend to have specific elements and a limited number of players. A professor said or tweeted this; students were upset about that; an administrator was quoted as saying something; a legal expert commented thus. Behind the scenes, meanwhile, many other players and constituencies are involved and ripple effects occur.

In my case, as I mentioned at the beginning of this chapter, the professor in question wrote an article that was perceived as being (and in my personal opinion, unstated at the time, was) severely critical of the population and culture of the state in which we worked. Many people were upset. This is an online/social media age, so the article—or stormy quotes about the article—were passed on and on until it seemed like practically everybody in the state and beyond was commenting negatively. One area of potential direct harm was our relationship with our alumni in general, but specifically alumni who were or could be major donors. Not surprising, quite a number of them were riled up. In my recollection, I ended up phoning at least a hundred people, and visiting—as in driving or getting on a plane—to meet about half a dozen to engage in damage control.

At this point, I am trying to interject nuance that takes into account my "J-school" heritage as well. So my version of damage control was different than for a dean of a college of engineering or a chair of a music department. Basically, what I heard from alumni was not that different from what I saw in the traditional media and online. These are also the kinds of statements that encapsulate public reaction to a lot of campus speech controversies:

- "It's just outrageous that we pay people a hefty salary and then they bite the hand that feeds them by attacking the good people of the state."
- "I can't believe the university has people like that teaching kids about what's right and what's wrong."
- "It's terrible that this is the kind of education students are getting in your program."

These feelings were completely legitimate. They could not be dismissed as coming from "outsiders not understanding us." The hurt was real, and while as administrators we feel a loyalty to our faculty, we also feel loyal to our students and alumni. The challenge is to balance these feelings. My personal ethic was to neither deny their right to outrage nor to throw blame on the professor in question. Instead, I made the case that

- We had many faculty members and they represented a wide range of opinion; and, in fact, a number of them took to print and online to disagree with the professor in question.

- We taught our students the fundamental American values of freedom of expression, freedom of thought, and academic freedom. Would you ask that we do anything else?
- There was considerable evidence that many of our students disagreed with the professor and did not feel intimidated about expressing their own views. No one was being indoctrinated or brainwashed.
- We taught and practiced the importance of healthy, vigorous debate on critical issues of the day, and that's exactly what was happening (Sableman, 1997).

In the end, I cannot put a dollar figure on the cost of the campus speech controversy in this instance, but every controversy can and has cost universities and programs potentially large amounts of money. And since a majority of the money donated to educational institutions goes toward student support in the form of scholarships, the ripple effect on students can be huge.

Another victim of a campus speech controversy, besides donor giving, may be the non-endowment portion of your budget. At most public universities, a substantial component of revenue to support everything we do, including faculty research and travel expenses, comes from undergraduate tuition. You can see the cases of entire universities, like Missouri, and smaller institutions like Hampshire College, where some campus controversy over who said what and when palpably reduced enrollment (Brown, 2018a, 2018b; Gardner & Patel, 2019). Parents and high school students are making a decision about the best—and, yes, the "safest" and most welcoming—colleges to attend. A program or a university that fairly or unfairly gets the reputation of being a trouble spot is less attractive.

In the short list of people who "matter" and who get involved in campus speech controversies, we cannot forget legislators and boards. We often hear only about the public statements uttered by, say, the chair of the board of regents or a few vocal legislators. But you can bet that the hotter and more prominent the controversy, the more people in power are forming an opinion and, behind the scenes, taking action. In the case of my nightmare campus controversy, individual legislators did make public/media comments and postings—although it was above my pay grade, as the saying goes, to respond to them directly. Other administrators had to worry about those consequences.

Then there is the general public (including advocacy groups) and media. My method of response to controversy was somewhat limited: I certainly was not about to get online and start exchanging views with thousands, possibly tens of thousands, of individuals. I did monitor social media, setting up my own Google alerts, specifically looking for instances where someone attacked our program (e.g., "So you are teaching our kids to hate their own state and people?"). I also responded to media inquiries; again, I think I was probably more voluble and contextual here because of my journalism heritage. I just couldn't bring myself to say "No comment," and typically made arguments like those listed previously.

I would be intellectually dishonest if I did not mention one other group affected by speech controversies, and that is academic administrators ourselves. Being a campus administrator today is a higher-risk occupation than it was thirty years ago. We live in an era when university presidents can lose their jobs because of the fallout from what begins as a localized controversy or problem on campus.

I know many chairs and deans who have given up on administration and returned to the faculty because of the stress they underwent when weathering repeated controversies. But public controversies are infinitely more stressful because of all the other actors involved and who must be addressed. Adding to the unease in my instance was the different (and understandably different) reaction by our president, who commented firmly on the controversy and wrote her own opinion essay in the same venue as the professor's original piece in which she stated, "I disagree strongly with and was offended by [the professor's] portrayal of Iowa and Iowans. Please know that he does not speak for the University of Iowa" (Mason, 2011). She was correct in her role and reaction; I hope I was in mine—but you just don't know.

I do not think I am stretching the bounds of plausibility to maintain that women and underrepresented groups are disproportionately negatively affected by toxic workplace culture (Andersson & Pearson, 1999; Cortina, 2008; Cortina et al., 2013; Miner et al., 2018; Montgomery, Kane & Vance, 2004) and thus may be less likely to seek positions where their own sufferings are magnified—for example, by becoming chair.

SOME TAKEAWAY BEST PRACTICES

There is no perfect set of actions for administrators to take when responding to a campus controversy because the situational details may be quite different from one case to the next. Furthermore, no one administrates in isolation. Other actors, including those at whose pleasure you serve, may tell you to do something different from what you want to do, and your choice may be either to comply or to quit.

There are, however, some best practices worth considering.

Take seriously the probability that at some point you will have to engage in crisis communication. The best way to perform well in a crisis is to anticipate it and plan ahead your range of responses and options of action. So you, as the unit leader, need to think about what kind of crises might occur and to prepare notes, maybe even extensive plans, of how you would deal with each one. The speech controversy is a single but serious example that you should ponder, gather expertise on, and determine your preferred courses of action. The worst thing that can happen in a crisis is for you, the leader, to be stunned into immobility because you thought it couldn't happen here.

Decide what your principles are and stick to them, including what you are willing to be fired for. While every controversy you have to deal with as an administrator has its own characteristics, it is best not to soul-search on a case-by-case basis (Pisciotta, 2018). Identify the professional values you plan to stand up for across the board, up front and in depth. If, for example, you decide that, in accordance with your principles, a faculty member's speech—whatever its offensiveness, perceived or real—should be defended, then defend it on those principles (al-Gharbi, 2019; Smith, 2002). Just know ahead of time (a) that it is highly unlikely that other administrators on campus will share all of your values, and (b) that there are potential personal career blowbacks and possible repercussions for your program and its students.

Respond quickly and factually—or as much are you are allowed to. Once upon a time, there was something called a news cycle. Leaders, whether in politics, business, or academia, had time to hold meetings and contemplate their response to a crisis. Nowadays, responses may be governed by external factors outside of your control, like Title IX or human resources (Thornton, 2017), but generally, speed is of the essence. Containing media virality is near impossible (Lindenberger, 2006), but the faster misinformation or miscommunication travels without a response, the more augmented it becomes. At the same time, you do not want to be so rushed that you get things wrong. Try to find out what exactly was said and what exactly happened before commenting. And keep in mind that other powers, like your boss or the university counsel's office, may directly order you *not* to comment.

Make the case for "American values" and don't argue the merits of the individual speech/text content. For administrators, it is seldom worth getting into a debate about the actual content of comments made by a student or a faculty member. You then become yet another interposing third party. Rather, if you feel that a matter that is handed to you or affects your program does indeed require your response, your defense of academic freedom, for example, should be just that: a defense of academic freedom. Do not get bogged down in minutiae and become another shouting head, in person or online.

About three years ago, a job candidate for a tenure-track position here at our College of Media & Communication asked me a question I had never been asked before: "Will I have to worry about what I say in the classroom?" She, like many faculty in our general field, addressed controversial issues in her courses. After all, our field writ large tends to deal with topics that are naturally more controversial than, for example, those that an accounting or horticulture professor may cover in an average lecture. We discuss religion in the media, climate change coverage, and interpersonal communication and sexuality, for instance.

My answer at the time still holds true—and has held true since she is now on our faculty. I said that my experience on our campus was that the vast majority of students and faculty are reasonable people unlikely to immediately take to the streets or Twitter when they hear something they don't agree with. Yet there was also a major caveat: we live in an era when no controversy, not even in the smallest classroom behind closed doors, can be contained and localized if any actor in the event does not want it to be. At that point, many people—including reluctant administrators—find themselves becoming a party to the conflict.

REFERENCES

Al-Gharbi, M. (2019, August 1). Noxious for tenure? Academic freedom was invented to protect scholars with reprehensible views. *The Chronicle of Higher Education.* Retrieved from https://www.chronicle.com/article/Too-Noxious-for-Tenure-/246855.

Andersson, L. M., & Pearson, C. M. (1999). Tit for tat? The spiraling effect of incivility in the workplace. *Academy of Management Review, 24*(3), 452–471.

Boyles, D. (2003). Joseph Kinmont Hart and Vanderbilt University: Academic freedom and the rise and fall of a department of education, 1930–1934. *History of Education Quarterly, 43*(4), 571–609.

Brown, S. (2018a, May 27). Mizzou's freshman enrollment has dropped by 35% in 2 years. Here's what's going on. *The Chronicle of Higher Education.* Retrieved from https://www.chronicle.com/article/Mizzou-s-Freshman-Enrollment/240136.

Brown, S. (2018b, June 1). Mizzou's freshman class shrank by a third over 2 years. Here's how it's trying to turn that around. *The Chronicle of Higher Education.* Retrieved from https://www.chronicle.com/article/Mizzou-s-Freshman-Class/243570.

Cain, T. R. (2018). "Friendly public sentiment" and the threats to academic freedom. *History of Education Quarterly, 58*(3), 428–435.

Cortina, L. M. (2008). Unseen injustice: Incivility as modern discrimination in organizations. *Academy of Management Review, 33*, 55–75. DOI: 10.5465/AMR.2008.27745097.

Cortina, L. M., Kabat-Farr, D., Leskinen, E. A., Huerta, M., & Magley, V. J. (2013). Selective incivility as modern discrimination in organizations: Evidence and impact. *Journal of Management, 39*(6), 1579–1605. DOI:10.1177/0149206311418835.

Di Domenico, T. E. (1995). *Silva v. University of New Hampshire*: The precarious balance between student hostile environment claims and academic freedom. *St. John's Law Review, 69*(3–4), 609–632.

Dobson, Keith S. (1997, November). The other side of academic freedom is academic responsibility. *Canadian Psychology, 38*(4), 244–247.

Gardner, L., & Patel, V. (2019, February 21). How Hampshire was brought to the brink: Distinctiveness has long been the college's calling card. Now it may threaten its survival. *The Chronicle of Higher Education.* Retrieved from https://www.chronicle.com/article/How-Hampshire-Was-Brought-to/245747.

Gruber, C. S. (1972). Academic freedom at Columbia University, 1917–1918: The case of James McKeen Cattell. *AAUP Bulletin, 58*(3), 297–305.

Huq, A. (2010). Easterbrook on academic freedom. *The University of Chicago Law Review, 77,* 1055–1072.

Lawrence, P. (2018). When core values collide: Diversity, inclusion, and free speech. *Association of American Colleges and Universities, 104*(2). Retrieved from https://www.aacu.org/liberaleducation/2018/spring/lawrence.

Lindenberger, M. (2006). Questions of conduct. *Diverse: Issues in Higher Education, 23*(21), 36–37.

Malek, A. (2007, March–April). Fifteen months after he enraged the Muslim world, Danish editor Flemming Rose's conscience is clear. *Columbia Journalism Review.* Retrieved from https://archives.cjr.org/q_and_a/beyond_the_cartoon_controversy.php.

Mason, S. (2011, December 15). Stephen Bloom "does not speak for the university." *The Atlantic* (online). Retrieved from https://www.theatlantic.com/politics/archive/2011/12/stephen-bloom-does-not-speak-for-the-university/250073/.

McDonald, J. G. (2005, February 10). Donors: Too much say on campus speech? Colleges feel more pressure from givers who want to help determine who'll be speaking on campus. *The Christian Science Monitor.* Retrieved from https://www.csmonitor.com/2005/0210/p11s01-legn.html.

Miner, K. N., Diaz, I., Wooderson, R. L., McDonald, J. N., Smittick, A. L., & Lomeli, L. C. (2018). A workplace incivility roadmap: Identifying theoretical speedbumps and alternative routes for future research. *Journal of Occupational Health Psychology, 23*(3), 320–337.

Montgomery, K., Kane, K., & Vance, C. M. (2004). Accounting for differences in norms of respect: A study of assessments of incivility through the lenses of race and gender. *Group & Organization Management, 29,* 248–268. DOI: 10.1177/1059601103252105.

Nugent, B. R., & Flood, J. T. (2014). Rescuing academic freedom for *Garcetti v. Ceballos*: An evaluation of current case law and proposal for the protection of core academic, administrative, and advisory speech. *Journal of College and University Law, 40*(1), 115–158.

Perlmutter, D. D. (2006). Hypericons: Famous news images in the internet-digital-satellite age. In Paul Messaris (Ed.), *Digital media: Transformations in human communication* (pp. 51–64). New York, NY: Peter Lang.

Perlmutter, D. D. (2008). *Blogwars: The new political battleground.* New York, NY: Oxford University Press.

Perlmutter, D. D. (2010). *Promotion & tenure confidential: The people, politics, and philosophy of career advancement in academia.* Cambridge, MA: Harvard University Press.

Perlmutter, D. D. (2014, December 2). Don't fear fund raising, part 4: Understanding donor intent. *The Chronicle of Higher Education*, 32–33.

Perlmutter, D. D. (2018, February 23). A crash course in crisis communication. *The Chronicle of Higher Education*, A25.

Pisciotta, D. (2018, September). 5 ways to avoid a free-speech crisis: Administrators walk a fine line when confronting the right to be. *University Business Magazine*, 21(9), 55–56. Retrieved from http://www.nxtbook.com/pmg/UB/UB_0918/index.php#/56.

Sableman, M. (1997). *More speech, not less: Communications law in the information age.* Carbondale, IL: Southern Illinois University Press.

Smith, S. E. (2002). Who owns academic freedom? The standard for academic free speech at public universities. *Washington and Lee Law Review, 59*(1), 299–360.

Thornton, S. (2017). Complying with Title IX while protecting shared governance, academic freedom, and due process: A model sexual misconduct policy. *AAUP Journal of American Academic Freedom 8*, 1–16.

Welbourne, J. L., Gangadharan, A., & Sariol, A. M. (2015). Ethnicity and cultural values as predictors of the occurrence and impact of experienced workplace incivility. *Journal of Occupational Health Psychology, 20*(2), 205–217. Retrieved from http://dx.doi.org/10.1037/a0038277.

Zamudio-Suaréz, F. (2016, April 11). Students were mad their college banned Yik Yak. So they went on Yik Yak. *The Chronicle of Higher Education*. Retrieved from https://www.chronicle.com/blogs/ticker/students-were-mad-their-college-banned-yik-yak-so-they-went-on-yik-yak/110285.

Part II

FOSTERING TOLERANCE

8

Flipping the Script

Difficult Dialogues and Blended Learning for Traditional and Online Journalism Courses

Marquita Smith and Mia Moody-Ramirez

In today's racially charged sociopolitical climate, it has become increasingly important for journalism instructors to arm students with the skills needed to discuss and critically dissect important social, political, and cultural issues. Difficult dialogues is the most common shorthand for referring to discussions of controversial and contentious issues. Classroom strategies often include modified debate, role-playing, directing peer conversations, small group discussion, and online discussion board use (Henderson, 2016). These methods of exploration mesh well with a blended, hybrid, and flipped learning method. While there is no standard method of sharing difficult dialogues in a flipped-course setting, students usually view lecture materials outside class and devote in-class time to exercises and discussions. Students have time to process and critically reflect on information before commenting publicly. This is extremely important as the goal is to develop more intelligent, critically thinking, culturally competent journalism and mass communication graduates, who are capable of positively impacting media coverage, workspaces, and communities.

Garyantes (2012) concluded that graduates seeking journalism careers need to better understand communities and cultures different than their own. The swift expansion of globalization, steady increases in diverse populations nationally, and greater access to digital technologies have created an environment that is primed for more inclusive storytelling.

To address media trends and a disruptive age, media scholars are recommending journalism courses that include storytelling through diverse lenses to support more accurate and inclusive coverage than previous decades (Gans, 2011; Ward, 2005). One way that students learn about the perspectives of those living in domestic and international communities is through the distribution of mass media, including news and social media content (Bennett, 2005; Brennen & Duffy, 2003). According to Garyantes (2012), journalists and media professionals continue to withstand criticism for their failure to engage in stories that cross cultural boundaries and report about the disasters and triumphs of diverse populations (Brennen & Duffy, 2003; Gans, 2011). To offer effective strategies for journalism educators to engage students in open discussions on hot-button topics internationally and nationally, this chapter explores how using the lens of critical race theory, journalism educators may combine difficult dialogue strategies and elements of a flipped or blended teaching model.

This study provides perspective on how engaging in contentious topics helps students to not only think more critically, but prepares them to better lean into diverse domestic and global communities. We discuss the learning approaches for journalism programs through two different courses: a gender, race, and media class course taught at a private university in the American South and an online advocacy class taught at a small private Christian university also located in the South. Both are essential communication courses necessary for shaping more well-rounded journalism and communication students. Findings and implications offer insight on this important pedagogical approach and successful strategies for flipping/blending communication courses that emphasize global controversial topics. Continued conversation on incorporating flipped learning strategies into communication courses offers the opportunity to advance and improve issue-oriented classroom engagement.

DOMESTIC CONCERNS

In general, U.S. media outlets have historically depicted women as passive and subordinate to men and people of color as lazy, criminalistic, and unintelligent. The coverage of ethnic groups demonstrates the manner in which dominant framing of "other" cultural and political groups within national boundaries has been negative and stereotypical (Dates & Barlow, 1993; Entman, 1993; Martindale, 1990). Sexual orientation also has been highly stereotyped. Gerbner and Gross (1976) argued that the media participate in the "symbolic annihilation" of gays and lesbians by negatively stereotyping them as "colorful" and "flamboyant" characters and dangerous psychopaths, although current portrayals are more normalized.

The 2016 election of Donald Trump as the forty-fifth president of the United States was cause for concern for many groups. The president's stance on issues regarding women, immigrants, people of color, and members of the LGBTQ+ community fostered unrest among many groups (Dates & Moody-Ramirez, 2018). Hate crimes in the United States increased in 2016, with a surge in incidents motivated by bias against Jews, Muslims, and LGBT groups, among others, according to FBI data (Berman, 2017). In a 2016 FBI report, the number of hate crimes increased that year with more than 6,100 reported incidents, up from more than 5,800 the year before. Most victims were targeted because of bias against their race or ethnicity (Berman, 2017).

Responses to Trump's election included a Women's March on Washington, a Day Without Women, and the sharing of social media content. The anti-Trump movement organized on Twitter under the hashtags #Anti-Trump and #NotMyPresident.

DIFFICULT DIALOGUES, FLIPPED
TEACHING STRATEGIES/EXERCISES

Social unrest is not solely a problem facing American media and journalism programs. Therefore, courses must address both domestic and global issues facing women and marginalized groups (Byerly, 2010; Geertsema, 2009). Globally, media outlets are reporting threats to democracies. Furthermore, several countries are questioning the legitimacy of national elections. For instance, the Spanish prime minister was not even elected, and the same for Venezuela (Graham-Harrison & Daniels, 2019). In 2018, Pedro Sánchez became the prime minister of Spain after his no-confidence motion filed against Mariano Rajoy of the Popular Party (PP) succeeded in Congress. The Venezuelan Electoral Observatory and the Citizen Electoral Network expressed concern over the irregularities of the 2018 electoral schedule in Venezuela, including low voter turnout, and the lack of the Constituent Assembly's competencies to summon the elections, impeding participation.

The effects of globalization and the impact of a disruptive age have had a significant impact on academia. Professors must adjust their style of teaching to keep up with trends. Hands-on exercises and outside activities, the hallmarks of a flipped learning style, have the potential to bring many positive implications for curricula and teaching methodologies. However, they necessitate rethinking how we teach the basics such as ethics, reporting/writing, critical thinking, and diversity.

Professors may enhance flipped or blended courses by incorporating new media, collaborative projects, and outside components while building on traditional literacies. Successful use of flipped teaching hinges on ongoing practical research and revamped teaching strategies to enhance curriculum and media trends. Such analyses have traditionally used a discourse analysis and cultural studies approach. Instructors may encourage students to focus on the production and reproduction of stereotypes through media. Media literacy strategies also focus on students' understandings of media's embedded ideologies and possible effects. Students must question the naturalness of media representations and identify hidden messages in the media.

Whether faculty members intentionally try to create a more inclusive curriculum or students raise controversial issues, the use of difficult dialogue strategies is also important for the classroom setting (Goodman, 1995). Having difficult dialogues with students has been examined by various researchers (Goodman, 1995; Landis, 2008; Ramasubramanian, Sousa, & Gonlin, 2017). Most conclude that the process of dialogue itself is valuable as it allows participants to challenge their preconceived notions and create shared meaning with one another (Landis, 2008; Ramasubramanian, Sousa, & Gonlin, 2017). The difficult dialogue approach is unique in that it "provides multiple voices, at different levels, the opportunity to enter the conversation" (Ramasubramanian, Sousa, & Gonlin, 2017, p. 539).

The two case studies in this analysis also used the umbrella of constructivism and critical race theory to explore how dominant ideologies serve to reproduce social relations of domination and subordination. Constructivist models of media education advocate the development of students' analytical skills while also allowing for independence and a role in the decision-making process (Knabe, 2004). Constructivism helps learners to internalize and reshape, or transform, new information (Grennon Brooks & Brooks, 1993, p. 15). In this framework, students are not passive receivers of media but active negotiators of the media with which they engage. This section offers exercises that journalism professors might consider when updating courses. Hands-on activities include perspective by incongruity, interactive theater, fishbowl, and circle of objects as described below.

Fishbowl. This exercise offers a discussion configuration in which a small group of stakeholders discusses a topic, such as culture, heritage, or diversity, in the center of a larger group of listeners. The instructor arranges the room with a small group of people in the center and a larger group of listeners in a circle around them. They prompt the inner circle with questions and allow them to freely discuss the topic or questions among themselves, while the people in the outer circle maintain a respectful silence, listen deeply, and observe nonverbal cues that carry meaning. At the end, the instructor brings the two groups into the same larger circle and allow them to discuss and ask each other questions (adapted from Brookfield & Preskill, 1999).

Using a book to explore cultural difference. These activities are used to help students consider issues represented in books. *Modified debate:*

Have students pick a perspective from a fiction book and debate a question from the point of view of that character or perspective. *Role-playing:* Cast students as characters in the book and have them play out a key scenario. Repeat the scene, changing roles and practicing alternate endings. *Small group discussion:* Introduce the concept of privilege. Break students into groups and ask them to identify instances of privilege depicted in the book. Reconvene the class and list the events on the board as they correspond to social location of race, class, gender, and nationality (Landis, 2008, *Start Talking: A Handbook for Engaging Difficult Dialogues in Higher Education*).

Circle of objects. This exercise respectfully acknowledges the varieties of cultural heritage and introduces visual and kinesthetic elements into a discussion. The instructor asks each person to bring into class an object that reflects something about his or her ancestry, cultural heritage, class background, or other feature you wish to illuminate. Give students several days to choose their object and consider their response. *Sharing:* Arrange the chairs in a circle around a low table. Invite each person, one at a time, to place their object on the table and to talk about its links to their culture, history, traditions, or other topic under discussion. *Tips:* Consider speaking first, to model the act of self-disclosure and to demonstrate a time guideline of two or three minutes. After that, let the students speak in whatever order they wish. Honor the silence between speakers (adapted from Brookfield & Preskill, 1999).

A research paper may be used as a culminating project for the course. Students are instructed to choose a topic that explores some element of mass media representations of women, people of color, and other marginalized groups. The research papers examine how marginalized groups have historically been represented by the media, followed by an examination of how these representations have improved or worsened.

Debate and honest reflections are encouraged, as students are encouraged to respect all opinions when offered.

METHODOLOGY

Researchers sought to answer this question: how can journalism and communication professors use blended teaching and learning to better prepare students to engage in difficult dialogues in their lives and careers?

At the nearly 17,000-student campus, a gender, race, and media course was taught. At the 2,300 (small Christian) university, students engaged in an online advocacy course. A total of thirty-five students experienced the blended/flipped courses. Data collection methods involved (1) observations in the blended web-enhanced class of the embedded case; (2) student interviews; (3) a student survey; and (4) review of documents and web resources. As with many case studies, the findings of this research are anecdotal and grounded in the specific case and have limited generalization to other courses. However, a vivid description of the selected case is attempted to help faculty determine if this teaching pedagogy would be useful in their journalism and mass communication programs.

Online Advocacy

Gathering support is vital to an organization's success; and when students combine advocacy techniques with online efforts, they can maximize the impact. This review explores how online advocacy students discover the many ways to target decision makers and how important it is to merge their current offline tactics with the power of online resources. Most students taking the course are interested in human rights, product development, health care, or political policy. The course's goal is to teach students to get the right message, at the right time, to the right people. About 50 percent of the students enrolled in the course were seeking a bachelor of science degree in communication, with a concentration in digital journalism and civic engagement.

For a portion of the semester, the class experienced is flipped. Their first exposure to new material happens outside of class, usually via readings, lecture videos, and other supplementary materials. Class time is used to do the harder work of assimilating that knowledge, through problem solving, discussion, or debate. After taking the course, students are ready for tough conversations. Students explored how social media have become a valuable platform for #MeToo, #ChurchToo, and the evolution of gendered movements.

Students also evaluated media coverage of the respective movements to determine missed opportunities for diverse sources. Students used outside multimedia platforms to monitor and evaluate faith-based conversations on disabled persons and the LGBTQ+ community. Allowing students the time to engage and reflect outside of the traditional classroom environment promoted civility and active participation. For example, students who monitored multimedia platforms in class used their reporting to write articles for the student newspaper on LGBTQ+ concerns in the United Methodist Church. Students working on the campus newspaper also published a series of articles on sexual abuse cases in the U.S. evangelical church community, and continuing sexual abuse cases at Catholic and Protestant churches worldwide. Student feedback gathered from interviews and course surveys is below.

(Student 1). The students did enjoy looking at others' campaign projects and blogs using the web-based system. Additionally, it was interesting to have more time to think about responses and ideas before posting in the

discussion boards. "I really appreciated time to get my thoughts together. I often fear sounding stupid when asked a question in real time." Additionally, students said unofficial and official feedback was helpful with improving their products.

(Student 2). As a newspaper editor, I had a wonderful opportunity to listen to what students were passionate about, and often they were subjects that aren't openly discussed in the campus community. #MeToo was an example of not realizing how many voices were missing from the conversation. Journalists still have the responsibility of taking deep dives to share people's truths. Only when I thought about how I could be a part of the solution did I imagine a role for me as a writer and reporter.

(Student 3). This course gave me the space to acknowledge my sexuality. When discussing Christian congregations and how members of the LGBTQ community are shamed and excluded from faith communities, I felt safe enough to share that I am bisexual. On our campus, I never thought I would have the courage or space to say that I believe in God and that he wonderfully made me.

Gender, Race, and Media

Using theory, critical analysis techniques, and personal experiences with race, gender, and class, students in this course examined the link between media representations, institutional practices, and how closely these images reflect reality. The course was designed to provide students with a basic understanding of the impact of media images and portrayals of individuals, groups, and society as a whole.

Early in the semester, students were asked to express their learning goals and to take an active role in monitoring their learning. Students also helped establish ground rules and decide how to navigate difficult conversations throughout the semester. Ground rules suggested by students were (1) be accepting of other opinions, (2) have an open mind, (3) stay on topic, (4) choose to disagree and still respect each other, (5) avoid judgement, (6) don't be afraid to ask for forgiveness.

In keeping with blended and flipped methods, students learned key concepts and theories before class. Prior to each class meeting, they read articles and viewed videos from the list of resources provided by the instructor. Typical class meetings began with a discussion on current events and news items emphasizing themes of gender and race, followed by student presentations and interactive exercises. In particular, the instructor encouraged ownership in learning and self-awareness in the learning process. Class meetings often included an examination of various types of media messages, guest speakers, and student-led discussions on topics explored in their blog entries.

DISCUSSION

Rarely is the first attempt at blending a course successful. Technology glitches are inevitable. Professors' low mastery of technology also contribute to resistance in many journalism and communication programs. Still, the authors of this paper highly recommend that instructors consider using either the flipped or blended learning model, particularly as a strategy to prepare students to engage in contentious debates, as well as preparing them to intelligently engage in culturally competent storytelling and media production.

When reflecting on the courses, we certainly agree with previous research that suggests the many advantages and challenges involved with blended teaching and learning. Just as the teaching model worked for secondary education in the United States and New Zealand (Zaka, 2013), we find that independent blended learning helped us to be more student-centered in our courses. We spend less time giving instructions and more time coaching higher-level projects in classes. We are able to help students process more controversial current events by allowing students to contemplate writings and videos prior to face-to-face engagement.

Blended learning and teaching helps both students and instructors develop new information and communication technology (ICT) skills. For professors with limited engagement with social media tools such as Twitter and Instagram, this provides an opportunity for creative student engagement. In one case, a student continued to actively post on a blog and students continued to share hot topics on Twitter a year later.

Based on research and teaching experience, we can give several reasons why adopting this model would make sense for journalism and mass communication professors. However, Bergmann and Sams (2012) warn against flipping a class just for the sake of doing so.

Rethinking how we teach journalism and educate communication students is required, but as we discovered it is a worthy investment for students, professors, and programs. We intend to help our graduates be prepared to speak truth in some of the most hostile communication environments across multiple platforms.

CONCLUSION AND FUTURE STUDY

In higher education, specifically in journalism and mass communication courses, further research is needed in how instructors can incorporate difficult dialogues into a flipped, blended teaching and learning environment. Higher education enrollments are decreasing, in particular, at private institutions such as the two highlighted in our case study. Beyond good pedagogy, this is a sound business decision for journalism and communication programs working toward creative solutions to serve a shifting demographic of university students. Future research could focus on how flipped and blended classrooms may help journalism and mass communication students become better global citizens. As suggested by Hall & DuFrene (2016), future research might also examine student outcomes of the flipped method to gauge its success. The use of technology and various types of activities is also important.

In conclusion, our students must be prepared to engage in a variety of difficult discussions, develop a keen understanding of people and the world surrounding them, and create media productions that give a holistic view, including diverse perspectives on an international, national, and community level. We believe flipped, blended learning and teaching is one strategy to help accomplish the goal.

REFERENCES

Bagdikian, B. (1983). *The media monopoly*. Boston: Beacon Press.

Bennett, W. L. (2005). *News: The politics of illusion*. Boston, MA: Pearson

Bergmann, J., & Sams, A. (2012). *Flip your classroom: Reach every student in every class every day*. Washington DC: International Society for Technology in Education.

Berman, M. (2017, November 13). Hate crimes in the United States increased last year, the FBI says. *The Washington Post*. Retrieved from https://www.washing tonpost.com/news/post-nation/wp/2017/11/13/hate-crimes-in-the-united -states-increased-last-year-the-fbi-says/.

Bramlett-Solomon, S., & Carstarphen, M. G. (2017). *Race, gender, class and media: Studying mass communication and multiculturalism* (3rd ed.). Dubuque, IA: Kendall Hunt Publishing Co.

Brennen, B., & Duffy, M. (2003). "If a problem cannot be solved, enlarge it": An ideological critique of the other in Pearl Harbor and September 11 *New York Times* coverage. *Journalism Studies, 4*(1), 3–14.

Brookfield, S., & Preskill, S. (1999). *Discussion as a way of teaching: Tools and techniques for university teachers*. Buckingham: SRHE and Open University Press.

Byerly, C. (2010). Status report: Global research on women in the news media. *Media Report to Women, 38*(1), 1–2. Retrieved from http://search.ebscohost .com.ezproxy.baylor.edu/login.aspx?direct=true&db=ufh&AN=48375304&site =ehost-live&scope=site.

Carter, C., & Steiner, L. (2003). *Critical readings: Media and gender*. Maidenhead: Open University Press.

Dates, J., & Barlow, W. (1993). *Split image: African-Americans in the mass media* (2nd ed.). Washington, DC: Howard University Press.

Dates, J. L., & Moody-Ramirez, M. (2018). *From blackface to black Twitter: Reflections on black humor, race, politics, & gender*. New York, NY: Peter Lang.

Dates, J. L., & Pease, E. C. (1994). Warping the world: Media's mangled images of race. *The Freedom Forum Media Studies Journal, 8*(3), 81–88.

Djerf-Pierre, M. (2007). The gender of journalism: The structure and logic of the field in the twentieth century. *NORDICOM Review, 28*, 81–104. Retrieved from http://search.ebscohost.com.ezproxy.baylor.edu/login.aspx?direct=true&db=uf h&AN=27768453&site=ehost-live&scope=site.

Entman, R. (1993). Framing: Toward clarification of a fractured paradigm. *Journal of Communication, 43*(4), 51–58.

Everbach, T. (2014). Women's (mis)representation in news media. In C. Armstrong (Ed.), *Media disparity: A gender battleground*. Lanham, MD: Lexington Books.

Gans, H. J. (2011). Multiperspectival news revisited: Journalism and representative democracy. *Journalism, 12*(1), 3–13.

Garyantes, D. M. (2012). At the community level: Cultural competence and news coverage of a city neighborhood. *Community Journalism, 1*(1), 47–66.

Geertsema, M. (2009). Women and news: Making connections between the global and the local. *Feminist Media Studies, 9*(2), 149–172. Retrieved from digitalcommons.butler.edu/ccom_papers/12/.

Gerbner, G., & Gross, L. (1976). Living with television: The violence profile. *Journal of Communication, 26*(2), 172–199.

Goodman, D. J. (1995). Difficult dialogues. *College Teaching, 43*(2), 47. https://doi .org/10.1080/87567555.1995.9925513.

Graham-Harrison, E., & Daniels, J. P. (2019, February 24). Venezuela: At least four dead and hundreds injured in border standoff. *The Guardian*. Retrieved from https://www.theguardian.com/world/2019/feb/23/venezuela-border-latest -maduro-guaido.

Grennon Brooks, J., & Brooks, M. G. (1993). *In search of understanding: The case for constructivist classrooms*. Alexandria, VA: ASCD.

Halbfinger, D. M., & Kershner, I. (2019, February 28). Netanyahu indictment closer as Israeli prosecutor seeks charges. *The New York Times*. Retrieved from https:// www.nytimes.com/2019/02/28/world/middleeast/benjamin-netanyahu-in dicted.html.

Hall, A. A., & DuFrene, D. D. (2016). Best practices for launching a flipped classroom. *Business & Professional Communication Quarterly, 79*(2), 234–242. https:// doi-org.ezproxy.baylor.edu/10.1177/2329490615606733.

Henderson, L. J. (2016). Start talking: A handbook for engaging difficult dialogues in higher education. *Teaching Sociology, 44*(1), 56–60.

Jaffe, S. (2018, June 25). Why anti-Trump protests matter. *Rolling Stone*. Retrieved from https://www.rollingstone.com/culture/culture-news/why-anti-trump -protests-matter-113934/.

Knabe, A. (2004). Constructivist learning perspectives in online public relations classrooms. *Prism 2*. Retrieved from https://pdfs.semanticscholar.org/4019/ d64092f92911051528116c7de36bfac9f6b6.pdf.

Krolokke, C., & Sorensen, S. (2006). *Gender communication theories and analyses: From silence to performance*. Thousand Oaks, CA: Sage.

Landis, K. (Ed.). (2008). *Start talking: A handbook for engaging in difficult dialogues in higher education*. Anchorage, AK: University of Alaska Anchorage.

Martindale, C. (1990). Changes in newspaper images of black Americans. *Newspaper Research Journal, 11*(1), 46–48.

Ramasubramanian, S., Sousa, A. N., & Gonlin, V. (2017). Facilitated difficult dialogues on racism: A goal-based approach. *Journal of Applied Communication Research, 45*(5), 537–556. https://doi.org/10.1080/00909882.2017.1382706.

Smith, B. (2000). *Home girls: A black feminist anthology.* New Brunswick, NJ: Rutgers University Press.

Ward, S. J. A. (2005). Philosophical foundations for global journalism ethics. *Journal of Mass Media Ethics, 20*(1), 3–21.

Zaka, P. (2013). A case study of blended teaching and learning in a New Zealand secondary school, using an ecological framework. *Journal of Open, Flexible and Distance Learning, 17*(1), 24–40.

9

Confronting "Bro Culture" in the Sports Journalism Classroom

Steve Fox

When I ask women about gender bias in the classroom, almost all have a story about being "talked over" by men—both students and professors. The classic workplace scenario is common on university campuses. One familiar situation: a female student will make a comment in the classroom (if the professor allows it) and then moments later a male student will make exactly the same comment and get applauded for it as if it's an original comment. Sound familiar?

This "invisibility" feature takes on new shape when paired with male students who raise and wave their hands to be called on during discussions. Add the tendency for many professors to ask male students for their input over women and a gender bias in the classroom quickly emerges (Jule, 2004).

In the early years of my teaching career, I began to notice my own tendencies to select males first during discussions. My awareness didn't happen overnight, and I credit women peers for pointing out the phenomenon. Once I realized I was doing it, I actively made a choice to focus on women in my classes and seek their input.

It's tough to quantify whether I've been successful, but I did have one student write on an evaluation that I favor women students in class. Needless to say, it can be a fine line to walk.

In sports journalism classes, which I've been teaching now for twelve years, the bias can be more pronounced. I spent about half of my journalism career as a sports reporter and editor, so it was no surprise white males dominated my sports classes. It's a profession overwhelmingly dominated by males in both the reporting and editing ranks.

In 2018, the Institute for Diversity and Ethics in Sport, which issues periodic report cards on gender and race in sports media hiring, gave the Associated Press Sports Editors an F in gender hiring. The report found 90 percent of sports editors were male and 88.5 percent of sports reporters were male (Lapchick, 2018).

When women do make it onto sports desks, they find themselves having to fight for respect from not only their colleagues, but also the public. I have one friend who now works for ESPN who tells a story about being a young sports writer and fielding calls from high school coaches on a Friday night. One coach refused to speak with her, demanding to talk to a male sports writer.

Meanwhile, women sports journalists are subject to vile attacks on social media—attacks that go way beyond what male writers face.

My goal from the start has been to find ways to get women into my sports classes and into the profession. The hurdles they have to clear are many. This chapter will focus on tips for professors (men and women) on how to navigate this gender bias minefield.

GENDER DISPARITIES IN THE CLASSROOM

After a career spanning more than twenty years of covering both sports and news, I was hired in 2007 by the University of Massachusetts Journalism Department. After being told there was a high demand for sports journalism classes, I taught two sections of sports journalism in my first semester. There were twenty-three students between the two sections, including four women. But in one class of thirteen there was only one woman.

This didn't necessarily surprise me at first. A good number of male students pursue sports writing after failed athletic careers. Meanwhile, it's been a challenge to recruit women into the UMass sports journalism concentration.

Why?

Too often viewers and readers view female sports journalists as the beauty queen sideline reporters seen during coverage of major professional and college games. In most cases, these women are capable reporters, but male viewers view them in a sexual context similar to the cheerleaders also seen on the sidelines.

But the love of sports is there, no matter the sex. What's interesting to me is how women reporters come at stories from a different perspective. The questions they ask tend to focus on the person, while men often are focusing on numbers and strategy.

Doris Burke is one of the best—if not the best—analysts covering the NBA. Jessica Mendoza has brought fresh insights into the booth on Major League Baseball games. The *Washington Post*'s Sally Jenkins and Liz Clarke remain two of my favorite sports columnists and I continue to follow the work of Kate Fagan and Jemele Hill since they left ESPN.

Women love sports. Yet gender equality remains wanting.

While the numbers have fluctuated over the past dozen years, classes have remained white male–dominated. In the spring 2019 semester, only two of the sixteen students in the sportswriting class were women.

Of the four women who took classes with me that first semester, only one remained in journalism. None remained in sports journalism. Pursuing a career in sports journalism means working nights, weekends, and holidays. For women there is even more pressure. They have to prove themselves every day.

My sportswriting class is set up as a bureau of sorts for the local newspaper, with students covering local high school and college games as part of their coursework. The goal is to give students real-life experience while also allowing them to build their portfolio.

I believe the class makes a difference. Currently three women alums are working in various production roles at ESPN, one is a beat writer with the *New York Post*, one has held jobs doing social media for the New England Patriots and the Minnesota Vikings, and one is a sportswriter covering the Red Sox and Celtics for a local website.

My hope is these successes continue. These women work hard—harder by far than many of the male students. I've also learned a lot about teaching this class over the past dozen years.

In a 2010 study published in the *Journal of Research on Women and Gender*, authors Tracy Everbach and Laura Matysiak touched upon the unique voices and perspectives that women bring to the sports newsroom. The pair interviewed women sportswriters to talk about their careers. All agreed women writers are able to get better stories from male athletes.

Joan Ryan, who worked thirteen years as a sports journalist for papers including the *Orlando Sentinel, San Francisco Examiner,* and *San Francisco Chronicle,* told the authors:

> There were many players that opened up more to women. I'd have conversations and get these great stories and columns because they would open up more. I truly was interested. You also could ask what was considered the stupid question, like, "What do you actually think about when you step up to the plate?" I think women are much more open to going outside the lines a little bit and sometimes players really responded to that. (Everbach & Matysiak, 2010)

When I started teaching, I didn't know what women students go through in journalism classes. The goal in many of my classes is to have students get out of the classroom, conduct real interviews, and work on real stories that get published. But putting women students into these situations also subjects them to put-downs, discrimination, and sexual harassment. On one hand, women are gaining knowledge by doing real-life field work. On the other hand, they end up in situations their male peers never have to face.

It takes a tremendous amount of courage for women to take a first step and enroll in a sports journalism class. Women know full well they won't be one of the boys. I now go into the first day of class aware of the air of male entitlement that permeates the classroom those first few weeks.

Bursting that bubble is job number 1.

BE DIRECT

Most male students who enter the sports journalism class are sure of themselves. Some are cocky to the point of being obnoxious. And why not? American boys are taught early and often that masculinity is built on playing and knowing about sports (Jule, 2004). Most come into class knowing they will never get paid to play, so they may as well get paid to watch and write about sports.

Most semesters at least three, sometimes five or six out of a class of sixteen students, have been covering sports for collegiate publications. It can be a little strange. The "bro culture" is palpable those first days/weeks of class. During the ten minutes before class starts, the battle of sports opinions runs high. One male student declared himself an "NBA expert" last year—at age twenty.

By the time they get around to taking my class as juniors, around one-third of those in class have already been covering games and writing about sports, so they've been with their bros a few years. At times, they will call across the classroom about meetings or assignments—leading me to remind them it's class time, not college newspaper time. It's a culture aimed at excluding women and others who are not part of the club.

For many sports-minded males, this locker-room mentality adds fuel to the entitlement they feel those first few weeks of class, which leads to my first tip.

Tip no. 1: *Practice zero tolerance.* I've become a lot more direct. Not obnoxious, just blunt. On the first day of class, I pointedly say the classroom is not a locker room or sports bar. I say I will not tolerate the locker-room mentality in class.

We discuss early and often the lack of women on sports desks and the great disparity in coverage of male sports versus female sports. I pointedly tell campus newspaper sports editors they need more women sports reporters and editors on their staff.

I will also stop class dead in its tracks if the male students offer any snide comments during any of these discussions. It's happened more than once.

A few years ago we were discussing the well-publicized 2010 harassment incident between an assistant coach from the New York Jets and Ines Sainz, a Spanish-language TV reporter. During a discussion about the incident, where the coach was throwing footballs to make Sainz jump, one student snickered. I cut off the discussion and asked the student why he laughed. I let the silence hang for a bit to make the point, then I discussed how even a little chuckle is unacceptable in the newsroom and the classroom.

Stopping this locker-room mentality has to be top on the list of priorities at each semester.

BATTLING THE "BRO" CULTURE

Many male students learning sports journalism easily find themselves swimming in the bro culture and believe they are more capable since they've lived and breathed sports since they were children. I've rarely had a male student who didn't compete in sports at some level.

Many women students have as well. I have one sports journalism student at UMass who has been a competitive swimmer since she was six and has known since she was a freshman in high school she wanted to do sports journalism. Another former student ran for the UMass track team, and another was a star high school soccer player. A student in one of those first classes played for the women's club hockey team at UMass.

They're all more than capable. But before women can even get a shot at their first job in a field dominated by men, they face direct and subtle bias from their peers in the classroom. The locker-room culture perpetuated by male athletes has in many ways been adopted by male sports writers and many male students. Making crude jokes and comparing sports knowledge gets you into the special club. But many women sports writers don't operate that way.

In a 2017 *New York Times* article titled "How to Help Kids Disrupt 'Bro Culture,'" author Ana Homayoun wrote:

> Bro culture uses the formidable elixirs of power and status to create a toxic social environment, and tends to be characterized by manipulative charm, entitlement and a so-called "rules don't apply attitude"—as well as an inability to express emotion, show remorse or be vulnerable.

It's the toxic environment we educators are looking to avoid.

Tip no. 2: *Bust up the bros.* Again, there is a certain level of directness involved here. For me, the approach has taken years to develop. It's definitely not comfortable.

It's best to look at it this way: teaching involves an intense level of concentration and when you're dealing with a class filled with males, focus becomes even more important. You want the women in the class to be comfortable and willing to speak up.

As a male teacher in this environment I feel obligated to steer the class away from bro chatter focusing on opinion and statistics. I instead try to foster discussion around storytelling, which is not only in the comfort zone of women students, but is also the direction sports journalism is moving. As ESPN and other 24-hour outlets dominate game-day coverage by broadcasting scores and highlights, the profession is focused more than ever on telling the stories behind the athletes.

Still, women students are nervous. I had one woman who wanted to take my sports writing class but didn't feel she could keep up with the men's knowledge. I told her what mattered was the ability to get athletes and coaches to open up and then tell their stories. She ended up taking the class and excelling.

Some simple approaches can take the air out of the locker-room atmosphere in the classroom. But you're contravening traditional teaching methods and years of patriarchal pampering. So start with small doses.

Tip no. 3: *Avoid the man-wavers.* We've all seen it during discussions. The guy or guys waving their hands, armed and ready to offer their opinions. Avoid them. The natural tendency of all educators is to select them. Don't. Select the women in the class.

In an interview with the *Chronicle of Higher Education,* Judith E. Larkin, a professor emerita of psychology at Canisius College, said her studies showed women don't like to be selected in class. Why? Because women "would be much more ashamed than men would be if they couldn't answer the question" (Supiano, 2019).

It's all about creating a safe environment. While it may seem counterintuitive, I believe calling upon women in class empowers them to speak up in all-male environments. If they continue in the field of sports journalism (and the hope is they will), being able to navigate a press conference or newsroom filled with men is a skill they need to develop.

GENDER DISCUSSIONS AND ALLIES

As I'm hopefully getting across the point that women in the classroom have opinions that matter, I'm also frequently discussing gender issues within sports journalism. Regular discussions range from the lack of diversity on sports desks in most media organizations to the disparity in coverage when it comes to women's sports.

I supervise a four-course sports journalism concentration at UMass and since the start I know I've wanted women teaching some of the courses. I've been lucky that two women have been teaching courses in the sequence. One of the courses, Issues in Sports, has been taught by a woman editor from ESPN for the past seven years. We also bring in women writers and editors as guest speakers.

It's important for both women and men to see and hear from women leaders in the business. I remain hopeful things will change, but getting these messages across in classes is a great place to start.

My sports writing class is not a theory-oriented class. By the third or fourth week of class, students are out on their beats covering games, writing stories, and live-tweeting. Unlike male students covering beats, women students find themselves subjected to conditions no learning student should have to endure.

Tip no. 4: *Sexual harassment WILL happen.* I do not say this lightly or for dramatic effect. For years I was relatively oblivious.

In the fall 2015 semester I had a student named Alex who came into the class bright-eyed, loving sports, and looking forward to getting on a beat and covering a team. For the final project, students had to follow a player or coach through the season and then write a feature story on her or him for the final.

I would regularly check in with students to see how they were progressing with their finals, but she kept deflecting, saying she was having trouble arranging interviews. When we began to get close to the deadline for rough drafts, this student still had nothing to show and the energy she had at the start of the class had evaporated.

She admitted she had delayed finding an athlete to profile. But then, when she contacted him, she said he followed up with sexual overtones, suggesting she come to his apartment at night so they could make out. That was followed by a series of drunken late-night voicemails over several weeks suggesting similar things.

I was a little stunned as Alex told me about the harassment. I shouldn't have been.

After hearing Alex's story, I checked in with a handful of women alums to ask if they had ever been harassed while doing assignments in my classes. They instantly responded with a yes (as they all laughed). Most of the upper-level writing classes I teach are built around the learning by doing concept. To hear I was sending students out to do classwork and they were getting harassed by sources was more than a little upsetting.

What bothered me even more is Alex initially didn't feel comfortable telling me about the harassment. I wondered how many other women students had felt the same way. Once she told me, I said she needed to stop communicating with him immediately and seek another student to profile. She was relieved and ended up excelling with another interview subject.

I also asked her if she wanted me to pursue the issue with the student's coach and the university. She declined. I asked Alex to recount the story. Here's part of what she wrote:

> It all worked out pretty well and the professor and classmates who helped talk me through the situation were incredible.
>
> To this day, after two years working in the sports media industry across amateur and professional levels, that's my favorite story to tell when asked about what it's like being a woman in a male-dominated field. I've been mistaken for a secretary, a fan trying to break into a practice facility, and a broadcaster's "young, hot wife," but those are comments you can brush off. That's the only instance where my ability to actually do my job was made difficult.

After Alex, I changed my approach in the class in two critical ways.

1. I'm up front about sexual harassment. Now, within the first few days of class, I very directly say there is a strong possibility the women students will get harassed on their beats. I say that if it happens, students need to tell me so we can figure out how to deal with it.

Two years after Alex's story, another student came to me saying an assistant coach she had chosen for her final profile was responding to questions over email and text with responses that included calling her beautiful or referring to her as "love."

This is what she wrote in part when recounting the incident:

> I then decided to text him back saying he was being incredibly unprofessional, [that] I am not interested in him and I am simply just trying to get an assignment done for class. He then stopped responding and I was completely sick with the thought of writing a feature praising him. Fortunately you said I didn't have to but when I think back to the situation I feel as if I should've . . . I don't know. Women journalists face this kind of harassment daily and they still have to get their work done.

In the fall 2019 class, several of the women students reported being cat-called while trying to interview players after games. There's no doubt harassment happens. The next step is reporting these behaviors to superiors. However, to date, students have been unwilling to do that.

I know I can't stop harassment from happening but one way to make it difficult is to allow for and promote group work.

2. As much as possible, I send students out as reporting teams. Where that falls apart though is during final projects. At that point, students are often on their own to interview a player or a coach for their final project. But if they're going out to cover games or other assignments, I send them out in teams.

Final tip: *Promote education and awareness.* One of the positives that came out of Alex's experience was that she was courageous enough to publicly tell her story to members of Women for UMass. The group funds student projects every year and committees of students pitch their ideas every fall.

One year after her incident Alex went before the committee for what was supposed to be a five-minute presentation and told her story. Stunned committee members spoke with Alex and a few classmates for more than thirty minutes. Alex's story helped the Journalism Department win the first of three grants, which we've used to fund and host the annual Women in Sports Media Symposium. The daylong event was held for the third straight year last April and featured Lesley Visser and Melissa Ludtke—two pioneering women sports writers—as keynote speakers.

I've been lucky to have many strong women impact my life over the years. My mother and my two sisters fiercely battled gender stereotypes. My grandmothers and my aunts—including my Aunt Catherine—were trailblazers in their own right.

At the *Washington Post,* I worked with fearless women who were visionaries in this thing we called web journalism. There are too many to name but some of the brilliant women I worked with there include Ann Thompson, Ju-Don Marshall, Carol Ritchie, Stacey Paloski, Christine Riedel, Chris Harvey, Jody Brannon, and Leslie Walker. Since entering academia twelve years ago, I've met smart women who have greatly influenced my thoughts on gender. They include Tracy Everbach, Katy Bartzen Culver, Sue Robinson, Michelle Johnson, Lori Shontz, Peg Achterman, Bethany Swain, Kanina Holmes, Gina Martino Francis, and my good friend and former colleague, Shaheen Pasha.

I've also had the good fortune to meet and work with top women sports editors and writers such as Jena Janovy, Joy Russo Shoenfield, Sarah Goldstein Lee, Kate Fagan, Melissa Ludtke, Lesley Visser, along with many others.

I'm hopeful for the future. The young women I've worked with in the UMass sports journalism program know the potholes and landmines in front of them, yet they charge ahead because of their love of the game(s). Keep an eye out for Alex Francisco, Mollie Walker, Sarah Corso, Kaitlin Boyer, Jacqui Collins, Shayna Hall, Sarah Jacobs, Allie Furlo, Bridgette Proulx, Imogen Fairs, and many others.

And, finally, there are my two daughters: Shannon and Kendall. Look out. They are smart and fearless.

They're all part of a new generation of women who will laugh as they crash through ceilings and stereotypes. No one gets there on their own.

All educators need to be allies to women students pursuing sports journalism as a career, but men especially. Many of us have been in a blissful sleep for a while now. Time to wake up.

REFERENCES

Everbach, T., & Matysiak, L. (2010). Sports reporting and gender: Women journalists who broke the locker room barrier. *Journal of Research on Women and Gender, 1*.

Homayoun, Ana. (2017, August 24). How to help kids disrupt "bro culture." *The New York Times*. Retrieved from https://www.nytimes.com/2017/08/24/well/family/how-to-help-kids-disrupt-bro-culture.html.

Jule, A. (2004). *Gender, participation, and silence in the language classroom: Sh-Shushing the girls*. Houndmills, Basingstoke, Hampshire: Palgrave Macmillan.

Lapchick, R. (2018). 2018 racial and gender report card. TIDES: The Institute for Diversity and Ethics in Sport. Retrieved from https://www.tidesport.org/racial-gender-report-card.

Supiano, B. (2019). How calling on random students could hurt women. *The Chronicle of Higher Education*. Retrieved from https://www.chronicle.com/article/How-Calling-on-Random-Students/246954.

10

Conflicted

Student Media Advisors,
Sexual Assault Coverage, and
Mandatory Reporting under Title IX

Meg Heckman

Student news organizations have a long and laudable history of tackling serious, complex stories that, in many cases, university administrators would rather they ignore. That can put the journalism professors who advise these publications in precarious positions where they may be forced to make a difficult choice: censor their students or risk losing their jobs. This conflict is especially apparent when student reporters cover allegations of rape and other forms of sexual misconduct. When that happens, college media advisors must be ready to balance their sometimes-conflicting duties to protect journalistic freedom while also satisfying increasingly common institutional policies that make them mandatory reporters under federal Title IX requirements.

Passed in 1972, Title IX forbids educational institutions receiving federal funds from discrimination based on sex and has been credited with improving conditions for women on sports fields and in classrooms. Although the law wasn't initially intended to address sexual misconduct, its scope has expanded in the nearly five decades since its passage and allegations of campus sexual misconduct are often addressed under Title IX. This evolution has "resulted in far stronger support for survivors, but it has also introduced ambiguities that leave room for misinterpretation" (Breslow, 2017, para. 3). In a growing number of cases, university administrators have applied Title IX in ways free press advocates say threatens journalistic freedom. "The intent of Title IX . . . was pure: end sex discrimination in academia. But an unintended and unexpected outcome of broad interpretation of the law may be a chilling effect on student press"

(DeWulf, 2016, para. 1). According to the Student Press Law Center, administrators have invoked the law to stymie student reporting by blocking access to open records and accusing student editors of committing sexual harassment for publishing content some readers found offensive.

There's also growing anecdotal evidence that interpretation of Title IX is complicating the roles of some student media advisors. In response to federal guidelines issued by the Obama administration, most colleges and universities have adopted policies that make all employees mandatory reporters under Title IX. The specifics differ among institutions but, in general, faculty members are required to immediately alert campus administrators of any allegations of sexual misconduct, even if that means violating a survivor's desire to remain anonymous (Brown, 2018). At some institutions, faculty members may be required to report information they hear second or thirdhand. Most policies include exemptions for clergy members and mental health workers—but not journalists. And that puts student media advisors in precarious positions. If, for instance, a student reporter mentions she received a tip about a botched rape investigation, you may have to alert administrators immediately. While it may seem fairly harmless to tell the Title IX office that a story about sexual assault is in the works, doing so could diminish the reporter's ability to do her job, especially if the people accused of misconduct are in positions of power. But not relaying the information may carry serious consequences, too. That was the case at Tarleton State University, a public institution in North Texas where student newspaper advisor Dan Malone was disciplined in 2018 for what the school said was a failure to uphold his duty as a mandatory reporter. According to school administrators, he was contractually obligated to immediately alert them when he learned his students were working on a story about sexual harassment allegations against a professor. Malone, a Pulitzer Prize winner who used to work at the *Dallas Morning News*, contends that doing so would have compromised confidential sources (Miller, 2018). Malone continues to serve on the journalism faculty at Tarleton but told the *Texas Monitor* that he now counsels students to keep him out of the loop when it comes to many aspects of stories related to sexual misconduct (Miller, 2019).

Some professional journalists working at university-affiliated public radio stations are also grappling with the repercussions of mandatory reporting requirements. In the fall of 2019, the staff of NPR Illinois was ordered by a University of Illinois Title IX coordinator to share confidential tips after it published an investigation documenting the "covert ways in which the university has dealt with accusations of sexual misconduct against professors" (Otwell & Mierjeski, 2019, p. 8). The university argued that because it held the station's license, newsroom employees were subject to the school's mandatory reporter policy. Station management pushed back, asking for an exemption for journalists. The school refused, arguing that the requirement did not "violate any constitutional or other legal protections" (Ornstein, 2019, p. 14). NPR Illinois's investigation into campus sexual misconduct is part of a partnership with *ProPublica*'s Local Reporting Network; editors there announced steps to protect confidential sources by screening tips and barring the station from accessing any that might trigger the mandatory reporting requirement (Ornstein, 2019).

The situation in Texas, meanwhile, became more dire for student media advisors in late 2019 when the state enacted a law that broadened mandatory reporting requirements under Title IX and carried criminal penalties for anyone who fails to comply. The new regulations have student press advocates worried (Miller, 2019), especially given that there are few if any court cases addressing the intersection of Title IX and the First Amendment. It's also unclear if other states are considering similar legislation. Free press advocates have long championed policies that protect the campus press, but, in practice, "student journalists and their faculty advisors work in a gray zone of legal uncertainty. While the Supreme Court has been generally protective of First Amendment rights at public colleges and universities, the justices have never squarely addressed whether college and university journalists have rights comparable to those of nonstudent professionals" (AAUP, 2016, p. 7). Advisors face an even murkier legal picture. A handful of states have laws that explicitly protect journalism advisors from retaliation, but such protections remain rare (AAUP, 2016).

The legal landscape may be in flux, but one thing is not in question: if you advise student journalists, there's a very good chance you'll grapple with this issue. Roughly 11 percent of all college students have experienced sexual assault, making sexual violence more prevalent than other campus crimes (RAINN, 2019). As a result, it's fairly common for student news organizations to pursue stories about this issue. In the wake of the #MeToo movement and sexual assault allegations against high-profile figures like Supreme Court Justice Brett Kavanaugh, student editors may be even more motivated to address rape culture as both a persistent social problem and as it relates to specific events on their campuses. Their work in this area is an example of the vital watchdog role traditionally played by the collegiate press (Armstrong, 2018). It's also becoming more common for student-staffed publications to serve off-campus audiences. In regions where local news organizations are struggling or nonexistent, student journalists are often called upon to fill information gaps (Francisco, Lenhoff, & Schudson, 2012). This means student reporting may be the only way some members of the public learn about allegations of sexual assault in their communities.

Threats of institutional retaliation for controversial stories aren't new. "Censorship of student media is not unique to the twenty-first century. Student newspapers have been subject to it since they began" (Armstrong, 2018, p. 23). According to one survey conducted in the early 1990s, roughly 20 percent of the advisors interviewed said they had been threatened with firing or other administrative sanctions as a result of material published by the campus press (Bodle, 1993). A more recent study conducted by the College Media Association (CMA) heard from more than twenty media advisors who, between 2013 and 2016, had encountered administrative pressure to censor student journalists. "This pressure was reported from every segment of higher education and from every institutional type: public and private, four-year and two-year, religious and secular" (AAUP, 2016, p. 1). And it wasn't just controversial topics that drew administrative ire. One advisor was ordered to rein in a student newspaper because administrators didn't like a story it published about popular places to have casual sex on campus. (AAUP, 2016). (It's also important to note that advisors are often among the most vulnerable faculty members; two-thirds of advisors interviewed in the 1993 study were either pretenure or in contingent positions.)

"We really are the people in the middle," said Chris Evans, president of the College Media Association and advisor of the *Vermont Cynic*, the University of Vermont's student newspaper (Evans, personal communication, July 16, 2019). "The people I work with—sometimes in the next cubicle—may be the people my students are writing stories about."

For college media advisors and their students, the best approach to navigating these complexities is knowledge. If your institution has a mandatory reporting policy, it's important you understand and comply with its requirements. Local laws are another factor to consider. A few states have had explicit protection for student journalists on the books for decades. In recent years, the Student Press Law Center has helped grassroots activists convince more states to adopt similar legislation through its New Voices project. As of 2019, fourteen states had some kind of statute protecting student journalists, although many were limited to public schools. Not all of these laws protect advisors, either, and it's unclear how or if they might help a journalism professor accused of violating a Title IX mandatory reporting requirement. (For an overview of the New Voices project and a state-by-state guide, see https://splc.org/new-voices.) Many states also have shield laws that prevent journalists from being forced to disclose confidential sources, but these vary widely and may not cover student media (Peters, 2016).

It's also crucial to determine what type of publication you advise. The idea of providing hands-on reporting experience is rooted in the early years of journalism education in the United States (Armstrong, 2018), but not all of these news outlets are the same. There are two main types of student-staffed publications: student-run enterprises, such as campus newspapers or radio stations, and niche publications created by journalism educators for the purpose of providing students with experience. Although there's some dispute over when and where the first student newspaper was published, the concept dates back roughly two hundred years. Although it's typical for these publications to have faculty advisors, they are run entirely by students as either school-sponsored clubs or independent organizations.

Over the last decade, an increasing number of journalism schools have also launched in-house publications to help compensate for shrinking local news organizations and a decrease in the availability of internships. These are often referred to as teaching hospitals or digital practicums and, as Francisco, Lenhoff, and Schudson (2012) wrote, can provide valuable training for new journalists.

> There have long been many programs in which journalism students do internships at news organizations. These continue. What is new, however, is the proliferation of programs in which supervision comes from university faculty, with or without joint supervision from partner media organizations. In these programs, the students' primary base of operation is usually their home college, not the newsroom of an independent media outlet; and the student-produced news stories are often made available at little or no cost, either to partner news outlets, or to multiple news organizations that pick up stories from a school website. (p. 2679)

Although these publications feature content produced by student journalists, they are not in the traditional sense student media; in some states, they may have fewer free press protections, especially if they're operated by private institutions (AAUP, 2016).

Your role as a faculty member will differ depending on which type of media organization you advise, both in terms of day-to-day practicalities and the amount of influence your institution can exert on content. If you're overseeing a teaching hospital, you may be much more involved with student work, serving as both an instructor and an editor. You may do this alone or in collaboration with a professional journalist from a partner news organization. If you advise a traditional student news organization, your work should be closer to that of a sideline coach than a player. The College Media Association, which describes itself as "the voice of college media and its advisors," recommends that professors overseeing these kinds of publications avoid editing, approving, or otherwise interfering in content production. This allows students to gain confidence in their ability to function independently in a working newsroom; it can also help advisors avoid conflicts of interest between their roles as journalism educators and their positions as university employees.

When it comes to coverage of campus sexual misconduct, balancing those two roles may be incredibly difficult, but preparation and transparency can help make it a little easier. Here are some tips to help you get started.

1. Know the specifics of your situation. There are a number of factors that can influence the rights and responsibilities of faculty advisors. Here are some questions to consider as you seek to better understand your role: What is your institution's policy about mandatory reporting under Title IX? If your institution is public, is it covered under your state's open-records laws? What's the publication's relationship to the university? Is it an on-campus club? An entirely independent organization? A teaching hospital like the type described above? Are there any laws in your state—such as New Voices legislation—that explicitly protect the student press?

2. Seek allies and experts. If you're unsure how to answer the questions above or need more information, the Student Press Law Center and the College Media Association are good places to solicit help. Spend some time on their websites—https://splc.org/ and http://www.college media.org/— and if you still have questions, contact their offices. You might also consider getting involved with one of these organizations by attending a conference or volunteering for a committee. Another resource is the *College Media Review*, an academic journal published by the College Media Association that addresses the past, present, and future of the student press. Back issues are available at http://cmreview.org/. (If you're looking to turn your advising work into published research, the review is also a good place to submit manuscripts.) Local press associations and regional free press advocacy groups might be useful, too, if you have questions about state laws in your area. If you work for a large university system, reach out to your counterparts on other campuses to find out how they navigate their roles.

3. Provide your students with resources on responsible coverage of sexual assault. This applies to the staffers at the news outlets you advise and the students in the classes you teach. For an overview of recent trends—and maddening statistics that show male journalists and sources are largely defining the news narrative around rape culture—refer to a report by the Women's Media Center entitled *Writing Rape: How the U.S. Media Cover Campus Rape and Sexual Assault* (http://www.womensmedia center.com/reports/writing-rape-how-u-s-media-cover-campus-rape-and -sexual-assault). The Center for Public Integrity maintains an online guide to covering campus sexual assault. It's called *Reporter's Toolkit: Investigating Sexual Assault on Your Campus* (https://publicintegrity.org/education/ sexual-assault-on-campus/reporters-toolkit-investigating-sexual-assault -on-your-campus/) and includes a host of useful information designed to help students get started in their reporting. It also describes common roadblocks—denied records requests, missing crime statistics, unhelpful officials—and offers advice on how to overcome those challenges.

The College Media Association's website often features tips for student editors such as one article that suggested publishing sexual assault awareness stories early each fall to help educate first-year students (Schick, n.d.). Showing students how their peers at other institutions have approached sexual assault coverage might also be useful. A *Salon* story from 2018 titled "How Students Newspapers Are Tackling Campus Sexual Assault" (https://www.salon.com/2018/01/21/how-student-newspapers-are-tackling-campus-sexual-assault/) includes several good examples. And a 2017 article from *Nieman Reports* explores how professional journalists are learning best practices for interacting with survivors (https://niemanreports.org/articles/covering-sexual-assault/).

Remember that these resources, while useful, also contain descriptions of sexual violence. Be sure students know this before they start reading. You should also remind them that it's common for even the most experienced journalists to react strongly to difficult stories. The pursuit of balanced, objective coverage doesn't make us immune to emotions. Remind students that it's important to engage in self-care and, if necessary, talk to a mental health professional. For more on the impacts of covering trauma, visit the Dart Center for Journalism and Trauma online at https://dartcenter.org.

4. Articulate your role often to both students and colleagues. If you are a mandatory reporter under your institution's Title IX policy, be explicit about that fact—and its potential ramifications for journalistic independence—with the students you advise. Do this early each semester to make sure all of your students, especially those who are new to the staff, understand what this means. You might also explain that there may be other times when your role as a university employee may create a conflict of interest with a story they're pursuing. Contract negotiations are a common example of this, as are stories related to committees on which you serve.

"It's a complex issue," Evans said (personal communication, July 16, 2019). "We typically put a line between what students tell us and what administrators tell us. I would never share what I hear in a staff meeting with my student journalists. Similarly, if a student journalist tells me something, I wouldn't tell my boss that."

You should also communicate to your colleagues that you advise a student news outlet; you are not its editor or publisher. If they have a problem with an editorial decision, they should speak to the students, not to you. For further guidance on best practices in defining your role as student media advisor, see the College Media Association's code of ethics at http://www.collegemedia.org/site/ethics.html.

If the publication you oversee is a teaching hospital (as opposed to a student-run operation), be sure you understand how or if state laws might protect the work you produce. If you are a junior faculty member or working in a contingent position, make sure your chairperson understands the legal dynamics at work.

5. Suggest students build a network of informal advisors that includes professional journalists and free press advocates. Remind students often that both the Student Press Law Center and College Media Association can assist them with challenging stories, even on a tight deadline. It might also be useful to help them connect with professional journalists or First Amendment lawyers in the community. State press associations are a good place to start, as are regional advocacy groups such as the New England First Amendment Coalition.

"The message that should be conveyed to students is that if you need help or guidance, make sure you get it," said Justin Silverman, the coalition's executive director (Silverman, personal communication, July 18, 2019).

To help students start building these kinds of relationships, invite reporters and free press advocates to your journalism classes as guest speakers. Or suggest that student editors organize a campus event featuring a panel of local journalists speaking about an important community issue. "I would imagine every hand in a local newsroom would shoot up," Silverman said (personal communication, July 18, 2019).

Under modern applications of Title IX, you may be unable to simultaneously protect your students' journalistic independence and guide them as they investigate sexual misconduct on campus. They will, however, need help navigating the complexities of these types of stories. Use the resources outlined in this chapter to make sure they get the mentorship they need to fulfil their roles as watchdogs and truth tellers.

REFERENCES

American Association of University Professors (AAUP). (2012). *Campus sexual assault: Suggested policies and procedures.* Retrieved from https://www.aaup.org/report/campus-sexual-assault-suggested-policies-and-procedures.

American Association of University Professors (AAUP), the College Media Association, the National Coalition Against Censorships and the Student Press Law Center. (2016). *Threats to the independence of student media.* Retrieved from https://www.aaup.org/report/threats-independence-student-media.

Armstrong, K. (2018). *How student journalists report campus unrest.* Lanham, MD: Lexington Books.

Bodle, J. V. (1993). Why newspaper advisers quit: Stress and professional prestige. *Journalism Educator, 48*(3), 32–37. DOI:10.1177/107769589304800305.

Breslow, S. (2017). What Title IX could mean for student journalists. Student Press Law Center. Retrieved from https://splc.org/2017/09/what-title-ix-changes-could-mean-for-student-journalists/.

Brown, S. (2018). Many professors have to report sexual misconduct. How should they tell their students that? *The Chronicle of Higher Education*. Retrieved from https://www.chronicle.com/article/Many-Professors-Have-to-Report/244294.

DeWulf, K. (2016). An unintended consequence of Title IX. Student Press Law Center. Retrieved from https://splc.org/2016/10/an-unintended-consequence-of-title-ix/.

Francisco, T., Lenhoff, A., & Schudson, M. (2012). The classroom as newsroom: Leveraging university resources for public affairs reporting. *International Journal of Communication, 2677*. Retrieved from https://ijoc.org/index.php/ijoc/article/viewFile/1636/818.

Madison, E. (2014). Training digital age journalists: Blurring the distinction between students and professionals. *Journalism & Mass Communication Educator, 69*(3), 314–324. https://doi.org/10.1177/1077695814532926.

Miller, S. (2018). Protecting confidential sources in sexual harassment case is putting college journalism advisors at risk. *The Texas Monitor*. Retrieved from https://texasmonitor.org/college-journalists-and-advisors-need-to-protect-sources-on-sexual-harassment-cases-is-getting-them-in-hot-water-with-title-ix-rules/.

Miller, S. (2019). New Texas law on Title IX reporting leaves college journalists and advisors in a tough spot. *The Texas Monitor*. Retrieved from https://texasmonitor.org/new-texas-law-on-title-ix-reporting-leaves-college-journalists-and-advisors-in-a-tough-spot/.

Ornstein, C. (2019). University of Illinois told our partners they must share sexual misconduct tips with campus authorities. Here's how we're protecting our sources. *ProPublica*. Retrieved from https://www.propublica.org/article/university-of-illinois-told-our-partners-they-must-share-sexual-misconduct-tips-with-campus-authorities-heres-how-were-protecting-our-sources.

Otwell, R., & Mierjeski, A. (2019). At the University of Illinois at Urbana-Champaign, preserving the reputations of sexual harassers. NPR Illinois and *ProPublica*. Retrieved from https://www.propublica.org/article/university-of-illinois-urbana-champaign-sexual-harassment-professor-faculty.

Peters, J. (2016). Shield laws and journalist's privilege: The basics every reporter should know. *Columbia Journalism Review*. Retrieved from https://www.cjr.org/united_states_project/journalists_privilege_shield_law_primer.php.

RAINN. (2019). Campus sexual violence: Statistics. Retrieved from https://www.rainn.org/statistics/campus-sexual-violence.

Schick, D. (n.d.). College media editors: Do a red zone story right now to reduce risk of back-to-school rapes. College Media Association. Retrieved from http://www.collegemedia.org/news/cma_news/article_b1b64b7e-15be-11e4-b4f7-001a4bcf6878.html.

11

#NAJAEverywhere

"I" in Indigenous (People) Is Capitalized

Victoria LaPoe, Lenzy Krehbiel-Burton, and Rebecca Landsberry

More than six hundred tribes exist in the United States, when combining federally and state-recognized tribes, yet there is a lack of knowledge from mainstream media to academics to the general American about "Indian Country" (USA.gov, 2019; NCSL.org, 2019). Inaccurate sourcing and imagery plagues coverage; news outlets want to go by their standards versus sovereignty and ethical research standards. A recent example of this happened with the *Washington Post* in August 2019, where the *Post* cited a survey that gauged Native Americans' feelings about the Washington, D.C., football team's racist mascot without details about the methodology (NAJANewsroom, 2019c). It also alluded to a cause-and-effect statement that Native people believe sports team mascots depicting Native people are OK and therefore aren't harmful.

Meanwhile, the American Psychological Association has noted for years that mascots are both harmful to Native and non-Native people (APA, 2019). It may be challenging for some non-Native journalists to understand how to vet credible sources to produce ethical coverage. A colonial lens has appeared to make some non-Native people avoid the genocidal history, instead of attempting to address what they may feel unequipped to navigate. However, here is the bottom line: journalists have a responsibility to learn if they are going to cover a story. Professors, too, have an obligation to teach budding journalists ethical ways to cover all communities. The uncomfortable needs to become comfortable to be an ethical journalist; academia, sports, and entertainment do not get a pass. Reinforcing stereotypes and naturalizing erasure are not acceptable.

This chapter focuses on collaborative thoughts from leaders of the Native American Journalists Association (NAJA), a 501(c)3 nonprofit organization representing more than 550 members working in media across the United States and Canada. NAJA's mission is to empower Native and non-Native media professionals through resources and programs designed to enrich journalism and promote Indigenous culture (NAJAnewsroom.com, 2019b). NAJA defends challenges to free press and advocates for the accurate representation of Indigenous communities, developing media literacy tools and guides for educators, students, and others in Indian Country (NAJAnewsroom.com, 2019a, 2019d). The chapter will also provide ethical material that may be referenced within academic and professional settings.

ETHICS RULE: NO PARACHUTING

Stories about diversity issues show journalists' ignorance about minority populations and the issues that affect them. Reporters make repetitive mistakes, such as using one source from the community for the entire story. Expecting one person from a diverse community to speak for an entire community is rooted in racism and plays into one-size-fits-all stereotypes (LaPoe & LaPoe, 2017). Who is speaking for and about whom matters, as it affects perceptions, policy, and people.

Journalists, professors, and students must responsibly follow the Society of Professional Journalists (SPJ) Code of Ethics to publish, teach, or produce ethical content. Unfortunately, NAJA has noted a trend among non-Native news outlets: sending reporters to "parachute" into communities to produce limited coverage and then quickly returning to other reporting beats. Coverage of Indigenous communities shouldn't be limited to a single story or month, but instead should be discussed and covered all year. Native American stories are critical to inclusive, ethical reporting on the history and current state of this country (LaPoe, Tallent, Ahtone, & LaPoe, 2018).

For example, the protests against Keystone XL pipeline project brought in journalists from all over the world, many of whom were unfamiliar with Indian Country and left once resistance camps began to break up. Although the large-scale resistance camps have long since dissipated, *Native Sun News Today,* an independent Indigenous publication based in Rapid City, South Dakota, continues to cover their long-term impacts, both socially and environmentally (*Native Sun News Today,* 2019).

To assist with ending the unethical framing of Indigenous communities, NAJA has created a series of guides primarily focused on coverage published in non-Native media. This model lays an ethical foundation not only for news outlets, but also for journalism professors teaching reporting best practices. During her time at Louisiana State University, Ohio University, and Western Kentucky University, Victoria LaPoe has taught classes across digital media, advertising, public relations, ethics, and media diversity, and no matter the geographic location, Indigenous professionals are included as key experts within the syllabus for each of these classes, naturalizing many aspects of Indian Country and avoiding the "one-and-done speaker" for a month.

ACCURATE PORTRAYAL OF INDIGENOUS COMMUNITIES

Non-Native groups likely think of Native communities most often when it comes to holidays instead of naturalized as experts and participants of everyday life. From Indigenous Peoples' Day to Halloween to Thanksgiving, Indigenous communities are often inaccurately portrayed within media. The inaccurate characterizations are harmful and are often produced without education and/or exposure to Native communities, perpetuating stereotypes and ignoring the foundations of ethical journalism, as outlined in the SPJ Code of Ethics (2019).

NAJA urges news coverage to provide context that includes questioning explicit and implicit racism that appears when reporting on stories tied to holidays and sports teams. NAJA also advises journalists to end the use of all Native mascots and team names, with a special emphasis on those that are dictionary-defined racial slurs. Below are some facts and lessons to think about when teaching and covering these stories.

Indigenous Peoples' Day

Indigenous Peoples' Day, also observed in some communities as Native American Day or named for a local tribe, celebrates the Native inhabitants of this land, now called the United States. The day supports pluralism versus assimilation and resiliency to uphold tribal sovereignty. Some facts to remember:

- Indigenous people were not discovered.
- Indigenous people occupied North and South America prior to 1492 and are still here.
- Noting a holiday as celebrating "discovery" of Indigenous tribes is factually inaccurate.
- The recognition of Indigenous Peoples' Day is an effort to honor an accurate history versus honoring genocide and participation in the slave trade.

Halloween

The celebration of Halloween continues to produce egregious examples of cultural appropriation as it relates to "Native American costumes." Even with the best of intentions, reporters can be unethical in their reporting by referencing stereotypes or using racial slurs in storytelling.

In October 2017, the Norwegian minister of finance, Siv Jensen, attended a costume party at a governmental ministry (located in a state-owned building), dressed in clothing meant to represent a real-life Native woman (NewsinEnglish.no, 2017). In this example, the news organization reinforced a position of racism with its headline, "Siv's 'Pocahontas' Stunt Backfired," which effectively framed the news coverage with a harmful stereotype.

In contrast, the *Hownikan*, a tribal media outlet owned and operated by the Citizen Potawatomi Nation, published, "Native American Halloween Costumes Debase Cultures and Communities" on October 11, 2017, highlighting an example of the damaging effect cultural appropriation can have on identity and mental health as these relate to "dressing up" as Native people (Potawatomi.org, 2017). NAJA suggests referencing coverage written by Native writers, specifically by their tribe, when considering coverage of or participation in events connected to this holiday. A Cherokee Nation citizen, Graham Brewer, who reports for *High Country News*'s tribal affairs desk, wrote a recent piece connected to costumes. From Brewer's reporting, it is clear that he is focused on Indigenous perspectives to provide context (Brewer, 2019). He wrote:

> An Arizona lingerie distributor has quietly removed one of its most offensive costume themes from its website, following years of protest from Indigenous women. Yandy, which is based in Phoenix, had until recently sold nearly 40 types of Native-American themed costumes, which drew sharp criticism from Native communities and activists for reducing Indigenous women to sexual objects, as well as inaccurately portraying Indigenous culture. (para. 1)

November: Native American Heritage Month and Thanksgiving

Native American Heritage Month in November provides opportunities for coverage of how Native people across the country are recognizing and celebrating their communities (NativeAmericanHeritageMonth.gov, 2019). Parachuting is especially common in the lead-up to November. While largely ignoring coverage of Indigenous communities for the remaining eleven months, mainstream media and academia often produce one-and-done coverage that miss the nuance and critical context for an ethical discussion. The NAJA Ethics Committee has encouraged the use of their tip sheet for reporting on Indian Country during this season to educate and inform coverage throughout the year (Rave, 2017):

1. Cover the tribes in their respective areas by asking them how they celebrate the holiday, or if they choose not to celebrate it at all. Also, identify each tribe by name versus lumping all Native Americans together within a story or even a headline.
2. Write about Indigenous food sources for Native Americans in respective coverage areas. The Indigenous population helped the English settlers at Plymouth Rock survive and avoid famine, in part, by offering guidance and aid in the newcomers' first harvest.
3. Run a story on how educators can avoid the use and distribution of fake headdresses and "war paint" to students as "dress up" items in the classroom. This concept may extend and include unethical use and naturalization of words associated with Native people such as "powwow," "off the reservation," "low on the totem pole," "hold down the fort," and so on. A strong story could include input from a tribal scholar or cultural leader in the region about these issues. The holiday also brings an opportunity for news outlets to discuss the beauty of traditional Native American clothing and art as well as Native contributions to the history of the United States.
4. Avoid referring to Native people as "figures from the past." For example, in 2013, the *Reporter* (2013) in Landsdale, Pennsylvania, published the headline: "Walton Farms Fifth Graders Bring Native American Tribes to Life." Instead, write stories and headlines with the context that tribes have living cultures that are vibrant and evolving today.
5. Produce stories that avoid mistruths that have formed and flourished over the years in stories about "the First Thanksgiving." Oyate, a California-based educational and cultural organization, outlines some of the myths in the article "Deconstructing the Myths of 'The First Thanksgiving'" (Dow, 2006).

Lastly, realize that everyone is not happy about this day. For many in the Wampanoag Nation, documented as meeting with the pilgrims, it is a day of mourning. Below is an excerpt from Michelle Tirado's piece published by *Indian Country Today* (Tirado, 2011).

> While today Thanksgiving is one of our nation's favorite holidays, it has a far different meaning for many Wampanoag, who now number between 4,000 and 5,000. Turner said, "For the most part, Thanksgiving itself is a day of mourning for Native people, not just Wampanoag people." (para. 9)

From those training journalists to those working in newsrooms, all forms of reporters are encouraged to review NAJA's Reading Red Report resource page for specific examples of how to produce ethical coverage: https://najanewsroom.com/reading-red-report/.

KNOW HOW TO APOLOGIZE AND
DON'T BE AFRAID TO ASK FOR HELP

It is the job of journalists and other truth-seekers to look at facts from multiple perspectives and attribute that as such. However, to be inclusive, there are instances when reporters must acknowledge and apologize for mistakes. For example, in January of 2019, an NPR reporter was quoted as doubling down on a story he produced earlier in December on the Indian Child Welfare Act (Jensen, 2019). However, NAJA released a statement including the following: "NPR violated its ethics policy by failing to thoroughly fact check its reporting and allowing racist language and views on air unchallenged" (NAJAnewsroom, 2018, para. 2). After NAJA contacted the radio network, NPR's Public Editor issued an opinion piece discussing the debate. A main issue of the coverage was the following: are Native people a racial designation or a political one? The primary problem at hand was a law about Native children and who can adopt them. As *Indian Country Today* reporter KickingWoman writes about the Indian Child Welfare Act (ICWA), "The law states when a Native child is up for adoption, homes of family or tribal members are prioritized for placement" (KickingWoman, 2019, para. 4). Interpreting tribal designation as race based, a federal Texas judge ruled ICWA unconstitutional (Kicking-Woman, 2019). However, in August 2019, a federal appeals court upheld the political classification and overturned the lower court's decision to strike ICWA down (KickingWoman, 2019). If a journalist finds themselves in this sort of reporting debate, we recommend the following approach.

Often, the best solution to understanding something new is sitting down, putting yourself aside, and listening to *hear* instead of to respond. If community members point out that reporters or outlets got something wrong, consider saying "I'm sorry" and listening. Here is how:

1. Recognize you may have made a mistake.
2. Apologize for the mistake.
3. Listen to the Indigenous community you may have harmed to avoid making the same mistake again.
4. Connect with appropriate groups for support and resources, such as NAJA.
5. Consider attending professional development workshops and conferences to learn best practices and connect with diverse communities in person.

Lastly, while social media may be great for finding sources, it is not necessarily great for solving conflict. Twitter brawls risk making all parties appear unprofessional. A better way is to reach out directly to people, meeting them face-to-face, whether in person or via digital tools.

ACADEMIC COLLABORATION

Anyone may become a NAJA member, and there are different levels of membership. Universities may join as sustaining institutional members—a level of commitment to Indigenous journalism that will assist with university programs and allow for close NAJA collaboration. As sustaining members, colleges such as Ohio University have hosted and sponsored a Native American Journalism Fellow, who visits the university to meet people face-to-face and who later attends NAJA's National Native Media Conference. Another option: perhaps your university has a high school workshop already in place. You can apply to become a NAJA student chapter and/or receive curriculum to certify your high school workshop as part of NAJA's Project Phoenix. For more information, go to najanewsroom.com.

NAJA RESOURCES

AP Style Guide Insert: https://najanewsroom.com/ap-style-insert/
Bingo Card: https://najanewsroom.com/bingo-card/
Indigenous Investigative Collective: https://najanewsroom.com/2019/02/11/naja-launches-indigenous-investigative-collective/
Reporting Guides: https://najanewsroom.com/reporting-guides/
Red Press Initiative: https://najanewsroom.com/2019/04/09/naja-launches-survey-to-assess-press-freedom-in-indian-country/
Student Chapters: https://najanewsroom.com/college-chapters/

CLASSROOM EXERCISES

Some classroom exercises that have worked well at an international level have included the following:

1. Utilize the NAJA bingo card (see NAJA resource list) to evaluate Native versus non-Native presses' news coverage. This would include looking at news organizations such as *High Country News*, which has a tribal affairs desk, and comparing coverage to a press that does not include tribal experts in terms of sourcing, visuals, and breadth of coverage.
2. Tristan Ahtone, the 2018–2019 NAJA president and editor of *High Country News's* tribal affairs desk, has asked journalists on his team to evaluate the negative within a feature story. He then asks them to think of something positive associated with the story. Often, even research is conducted from a colonial negative lens. We must question how stories are composed and how we know *what we think we know* in terms of facts (CNAIR, 2019).

3. Believe your eyes: for example, in the aftermath of the January 2019 conflict in Washington, D.C., between a Kentucky high school student and an Omaha Nation elder, Nathan Phillips, the mainstream media questioned and perpetuated the narrative that reporters shouldn't believe their own eyes, despite video that emerged showing students mocking Phillips with tomahawk chops (Ahtone, 2019). Ohio University professor Victoria LaPoe conducted an exercise that evaluated assumptions and terms within student media editorials. She went line-by-line through the students' articles and asked about the source and context of each fact. This resulted in an independent student media group on campus establishing equal space and sourcing obligations when building arguments as fact. The student media editor met with LaPoe and held two emergency staff meetings to develop quality check guidelines. Following the publication of an improperly sourced editorial by a new beginning writer, it was clear that there was a faulty perception that triggered the unsourced, assumed editorial. There was a belief that the newsroom contained mostly "liberal students," so they needed a "conservative" point of view for "balanced" coverage. What resulted was stereotypically framed, one-sided coverage.

4. Evaluate your own coverage: after students publish news coverage on Indigenous issues at the university, LaPoe works with students to evaluate the coverage utilizing NAJA guidelines and resources. The postmortem evaluation for students is just as important as the preparation, as you can see what didn't stick with students from previous NAJA ethics trainings. When professional news organizations make major errors in coverage, NAJA brings it to the organization's attention, but also offers education and ethics training. This process of evaluation is not about blame, but about moving the ethical needle forward in covering Indian Country.

5. Train students to follow other guides than just the *AP Stylebook*. NAJA recommends capitalizing all references to "Indigenous" when referring to people; however, this recommendation is still missing from the *AP Stylebook* (NAJAnewsroom.com, 2019a). Many tribal media outlets have adopted it as an ethical standard. Using the capitalizations shows that the news story is referencing real people with real identities.

6. Feature NAJA speakers' expertise in the classroom. Require students to research their work; submit two questions before they speak; share those questions with speakers; and then have students write or tweet what they have learned. If putting on social media, confirm appropriate tags and context with speakers.

7. Host an event with NAJA. Below is one exercise completed in November 2018 at a NAJA national reporting event held at Ohio University; the university had a rash of sexual assaults and students needed a place to discuss reporting.

Covering sexual assault
in Indian Country and beyond

With keynote speaker, Mary Annette Pember

Wednesday, November 14, 2018
7:30 pm
Schoonover Hall
Room 145

Mary Annette Pember, an award-winning Indigenous journalist and expert on covering sexual assault, trauma, policy, health and the environment, will advise students and attendees on how to cover sexual assault cases and share expert thoughts on coverage of violence against women.

Pember is an enrolled member of the Red Cliff Band of Wisconsin Ojibwe tribe and an independent journalist focused on Native American issues. Her reporting has covered important stories including the high rates of sexual assault among Native women, sex trafficking, health, impact of historical trauma on Native communities, environmental challenges on Native lands, federal policy issues as well as cultural and spiritual topics.

She is a past president and executive director of the Native American Journalists Association, and the 2018 Medill Milestone Achievement Award recipient. She has won industry awards and fellowships from the International Center for Journalism, Women in Communications, The Associated Press, USC Annenberg, the Carter Center, the University of Maryland and others.

Her keynote address will be followed by a panel of students, Dr. Patty Stokes of WGSS, who has expertise in the prevention and aftermath of sexual assault, and WOUB Editor-In-Chief Allison Hunter.

The event will be streamed live on **https://acrn.com**

After the panel, refreshments and beverages will be provided.

The Native American Journalists Association is proud to co-host this event with Ohio University, the E. W. Scripps School of Journalism, the Scripps College of Communication, and the Institute for Applied and Professional Ethics. For more information, please contact us at naja.com.

Figure 11.1. Flyer for national NAJA event held in partnership with Ohio University.

Dr. LaPoe's Directions to the Exercise:
Share on social media two things you learned from the event "Covering Sexual Assault in Indian Country and Beyond." If you follow instructions and are accurate and ethical, this may be a good resume builder for you on covering events as they happen on social media.

For your assignment, please share on Twitter: #VAWA #NAJAEverywhere, and #oujour2500. Please tag @najournalists. You can tweet or connect on other social media platforms to non-Native media, professional and student chapter orgs like SPJ (@SPJ_tweets), and others with #didyouknow. Tweet facts and information as relevant. You can also put images on Instagram with the above tags and mentions. There are many partners for this event to mention within your posts.

See the press release below and note that this is a NAJA national event held at Ohio University: https://www.ohio.edu/scrippscollege/newsevents/news-story.cfm?newsItem=60197839-5056-A874-1D8777CD5154EF9C.

I'd encourage you to review NAJA resource guides such as the bingo card, NAJA AP Style guide, and Indigenous Terminology Guide. If you like sharing messages of this event in this way, you may do more than two posts for additional credit. You may also tweet promotions for this event to remind students and others to tune in or attend.

You are expected to be ethical and to follow PRSSA [Public Relations Student Society of America] or SPJ code of ethics, depending on your role. Are you promoting, similar to a newsroom sharing upcoming news stories (SPJ code of ethics)? Or are you promoting an event (PRSSA code of ethics)? Use appropriate ethics codes as guidelines.

You may find good examples of covering events with Twitter by reviewing the following feeds:

- @tahtone—Tristan Ahtone, NAJA President, who spoke to the class, has a couple countdowns on his Twitter page that are really effective.
- @lenzykb—Lenzy Krehbiel-Burton, NAJA Board Secretary, has excellent examples of reporting at meetings and other venues; oftentimes, setting the tone and providing context to what she is reporting on.
- @najournalists—NAJA's official feed has a good Twitter breakdown of #WeAreStillHere coverage.

Production and Programming Notes:

- OU's Sexual Assault Coverage event had more than a dozen sponsors for this national event held at a university, including many organizations within the university.
- The Violence Against Women Act (VAWA) was in news headlines and its renewal was up in the air. NAJA wrote, produced, and unveiled a reporting guide at this event addressing VAWA in Indian Country: https://najanewsroom.com/reporting-guides/.
- Printed NAJA resource guides were available for all attendees.

Program Breakdown:
There was a keynote address, followed by a student media panel moderated by the keynote speaker and a professor from Women's, Gender & Sexuality Studies. Following the keynote and panel, moderators encouraged a community conversation and several members outside of the university came to ask questions. More than 250 people attended and many stayed for more than two hours to discuss the content. The live feed on Facebook was watched more than seven hundred times. A media student was hired to produce graphics and livestream the event with a switcher that changed camera angles. LaPoe worked with the student and NAJA on preproduced graphics. NAJA also worked with the college and journalism school to produce promotional material, ensuring accurate and appropriately packaged information. New research on missing and murdered Indigenous women (MMIW) broke on the day of this event; Seattle's Urban Indian Health Institute provided a media toolkit and suggested social media hashtags. Information was presented as a background slideshow during the event so that students and attendees had time to digest the material.

Ohio University had been grappling with a string of sexual assaults that were leading headlines nationally. This event seemed to be helpful to students who wanted to discuss the recent events. LaPoe spoke with the office of Equal and Civil Rights Compliance at the university and read a statement, approved by the office, detailing resources and waiving the faculty mandatory reporter requirements.

The university and community sexual assault outreach programs had booths and staff set up before, during, and after the event with fliers and resources. In both an introduction to advertising and public relations class and one on digital storytelling, teams of students worked on covering multiple angles of this event, creating and promoting a plan for consistent online team coverage.

REFERENCES

Ahtone, T. (2019, January 25). The mishandling of the MAGA teen story shows why I gave up on mainstream media. *The Washington Post*. Retrieved from https://www.washingtonpost.com/nation/2019/01/25/mishandling-maga-teens-story-shows-why-i-gave-up-mainstream-media/?utm_term=.1e32032670c2.

American Psychological Association. (2019). Summary of the APA resolution recommending retirement of American Indian mascots. Retrieved from https://www.apa.org/pi/oema/resources/indian-mascots.

Brewer, G. L. (2019, August 18). Lingerie company Yandy quietly removes Native American-themed costumes. *High Country News*. Retrieved from https://www.hcn.org/articles/tribal-affairs-lingerie-company-quietly-removes-native-american-themed-costumes.

Center for Native American and Indigenous Research (CNAIR). (2019). Digital reporting in Indigenous communities. Northwestern University. Retrieved from https://www.cnair.northwestern.edu/about/resources/video-gallery.html.

Dow, J. (2006). Deconstructing the myths of "The First Thanksgiving." *Oyate*. Retrieved from http://bit.ly/1cHXyT8.

Jensen, E. (2019, January 23). Assessing an NPR report on the Indian Child Welfare Act. NPR. Retrieved from https://www.npr.org/sections/publiceditor/2019/01/23/687694348/assessing-an-npr-report-on-the-indian-child-welfare-act.

KickingWoman, K. (2019, August 9). Court ruled that ICWA is constitutional. *Indian Country Today*. Retrieved from https://newsmaven.io/indiancountrytoday/news/court-ruled-that-icwa-is-constitutional-IzM9Ib7M0U6YXgmh2UdBXA/.

LaPoe, V., & LaPoe, B. (2017). *Indian Country: Telling a story in a digital age*. Lansing, MI: Michigan State Press.

LaPoe, V., Tallent, R., Ahtone, T., & LaPoe, B. (2018). Ethics and reporting on Native communities: Going beyond the parachute story. In V. LaPoe, C. Carter Olson, & B. LaPoe (Eds.), *Underserved communities and digital discourse: Getting voices heard* (pp. 185–204). Lanham, MD: Lexington Books.

NAJAnewsroom.com. (2018, December 18). NPR airs inaccurate story about ICWA case. Retrieved from https://najanewsroom.com/2018/12/18/npr-airs -inaccurate-story-about-icwa-case/.

NAJAnewsroom.com. (2019a). AP style insert. Retrieved from https://najanews room.com/ap-style-insert/.

NAJAnewsroom.com. (2019b). Mission. Retrieved from https://najanewsroom .com/mission/.

NAJAnewsroom.com. (2019c, August 12). NAJA demands the *Washington Post* retract unreliable data sets and all associated reporting. Retrieved from https:// najanewsroom.com/2019/08/12/naja-demands-the-washington-post-retract -unreliable-data-sets-and-all-associated-reporting/.

NAJAnewsroom.com. (2019d). Resources for reporting in Indian Country. Retrieved from https://najanewsroom.com/resources/.

National Conference of State Legislatures (NCSL). (2019). Federal and State recognized tribes. Retrieved from http://www.ncsl.org/research/state-tribal -institute/list-of-federal-and-state-recognized-Tribes.aspx.NativeAmerican HeritageMonth.gov. (2019). Retrieved from https://nativeamericanheritage month.gov.

Native Sun News Today. (2019). Keystone XL pipeline. Retrieved from https://www .nativesunnews.today/?s=keystone+xl+pipeline.

NewsinEnglish.no. (2017, October 17). Siv's "Pocahontas" stunt backfired. Retrieved from http://www.newsinenglish.no/2017/10/17/sivs-pocahontas -stunt-backfired/.

Potawatomi.org. (2017, October 11). "Native American" Halloween costumes debase cultures and communities. Retrieved from http://www.potawatomi.org/ native-american-halloween-costumes-debase-cultures-communities/.

Rave, J. (2017). Native American Heritage Day is Nov. 24, 2017. *Buffalo's Fire.* Retrieved from https://www.buffalosfire.com/naja-releases-responsible -reporting-guide-for-november-related-coverage/.

The Reporter. (2013, November 18). Walton Farm's fifth graders bring Native American tribes to life. Retrieved from http://bit.ly/1aCyRrP.

Society of Professional Journalists (SPJ). (2019). SPJ code of ethics. Retrieved from https://www.spj.org/ethicscode.asp.

Tirado, M. (2011, November 23). The Wampanoag side of the first Thanksgiving story. *Indian Country Today.* Retrieved from https://newsmaven.io/indian countrytoday/archive/the-wampanoag-side-of-the-first-thanksgiving-story -TmMLTgQs40aJT_n9T3RMIQ/.

USA.gov. (2019). Federally recognized Indian tribes and resources for Native Americans. Retrieved from https://www.usa.gov/tribes.

12

Wait. . . Hold On. . . Just Let Me *Explain* This to You . . .

Laura Castañeda

Early in my academic career, a kindly tenured professor took me and another faculty member to lunch and went off on a tangent about how important it is for mothers to stay home with their babies instead of going to work. "Do you plan to have children?" he asked. I was speechless. But the third faculty member, also a tenured male, stepped in and said, "That question is irrelevant." And we moved on.

My colleague was ahead of his time in his effort to be a good upstander and use his privilege to stand up for a Latina assistant professor who was uncomfortably stunned into silence. You'd think that in the two decades since then that various types of misogyny would be regularly called out by anyone who sees them. But the problem seems to be getting worse (or, thanks to social media, we hear about the most egregious examples more than ever). Case in point: mansplaining.

Consider the case of the cis male Facebook user, tampons, and taxes. By the time this text is in print, there will likely have been several more hilarious, head-scratching, and infuriating examples of what it is to "mansplain," or what the *Oxford English Dictionary* defines as: "Of a man: to explain (something) needlessly, overbearingly, or condescendingly, esp. (typically when addressing a woman) in a manner thought to reveal a patronizing or chauvinistic attitude." *Merriam-Webster*'s description isn't much different: "to explain something to a woman in a condescending way that assumes she has no knowledge about the topic." You can also check the Urban Dictionary's definition of "mansplain" to get, well, mansplained about what mansplaining *really* means. By men. To men. Well, maybe you can skip that one.

In any event, back to one of the more curious examples of mansplaining, which involved a man on Facebook trying to stop women from "whining" about the cost of tampons. He incorrectly claimed that women only use seven to nine tampons per menstrual cycle, and thus only require ninety tampons "maximum" per year (Chen, 2019). At the risk of being called "difficult," last I checked, there are twelve months per year, and it is dangerous to wear a tampon for more than eight hours—toxic shock and all. But who am I, as a woman with a uterus, to question a man, without a uterus?

Sadly, this wasn't the only example of mansplaining to explode on social media. Just weeks before the tampon kerfuffle came the vulva/vagina fracas. Responding to a newspaper article about photos of vulvas, a man wrote, "The correct word is vagina." A gynecologist and "international expert on both the vagina and the vulva" responded to the man, explaining that the photos featured vulvas (the outside part of female genitalia) and not vaginas (the inside part). The man then admitted they are indeed vulvas but believes the word "vaginas" should be used. Oh, and he then explained "mansplaining." Matter settled, I guess (Altma, 2018, para. 9).

Reader, there's more. In 2017, a doctoral student in the UK asked women on Twitter for the worst examples of mansplaining they had experienced (Murray, 2017). Fasten your seatbelts:

nicole froio@NicoleFroio
Quote this tweet with the most obvious thing a man has ever mansplained to you.

WhereIs Darrell Issa
@WhereisTheIssa
Replying to
@NicoleFroio
How to put oil into a sauté pan. I'm a chef.

Yo-Jo
@notcreative_meh
Replying to
@NicoleFroio
I'm a geologist. I had a marketing guy mansplain that oil is the lubricant for tectonic plates & removing it is causing less earthquakes.

the spooky bi magpie
@punkvenus

Replying to
@NicoleFroio
How the life cycle of a butterfly works. I work in a butterfly house &
have a degree in biology.

Ariana Sigel
@arianasigel
Replying to
@NicoleFroio
How to travel in Italy and what the weather is like in summer. Sono
Italiano, io parlo Italiano, anche mia famiglia abita in Italia.

Belinda McBride
@Belinda_McBride
Replying to
@NicoleFroio
When a man explained to me that childbirth was no different than
pooping.

LEARNING OBJECTIVES

You get the picture. All snark aside, some of you may be asking what this
has to do with life as a student, staff, or faculty member at a postsecondary institution? To be sure, not all men mansplain. All of us have been
taught and mentored by outstanding male educators and professionals.
We've worked alongside brilliant, supportive male colleagues. Many
of us have the privilege of working with and teaching creative, bright,
and optimistic male students. However, we know that mansplaining,
although it seems like a minor irritant, can be one of many slights that
burden and eventually weigh down many women. The goal for anyone
reading this chapter is to help stop the practice. By the end of this chapter,
you should be able to recognize mansplaining, understand the origins of
the term, articulate why mansplaining can be damaging, and implement
strategies to reduce, if not eliminate, mansplaining in the classroom and
in the academic workplace.

HOW THE TERM "MANSPLAIN" WAS BORN

Although the act of mansplaining has been around as long as men and
women have been communicating, the term "mansplain" was first
documented by lexicographers in August 2008 (Ha, 2018). Two bloggers,

electricwitch and count-vronsky, were having an exchange on Livejournal about Mieko Shiomi, a Japanese artist. Responding to a question from electricwitch, count-vronsky wrote that a dead pheasant in one of the images was "a sly take on the Last Supper (and the first supper—water into wine)" and represented "an absurdist comment on woman's [*sic*] maternal role as food provider, life as chemistry, and the sexual imagery of the after meal smoke." Electricwitch responded: "Wow, thank you so much for mansplaining this art to me! What with my arts degrees, I can't understand it at all!"

Writer, historian, and activist Rebecca Solnit is often given credit for the term "mansplain" because of an infamous scene in her essay-turned-book, *Men Explain Things to Me*, where she writes about how a man at a party was aggressively explaining a book about photographer Eadweard Muybridge to her, and she unsuccessfully was trying to tell him she had written that exact book (Solnit, 2014). In fact, she never used the term "mansplain" in *Men Explain Things to Me*, and in later years admitted to not liking the term (Lewis, 2014). However, for better or worse, it became shorthand for a phenomenon that many women had experienced but could not articulate. "Mansplaining" became the *New York Times*'s word of the year in 2010 (Wilhelm, 2017) and Scrabble added "mansplain" and its thirteen points to its official list of words (Pandey, 2019). Over the past several years, the term has given rise to many others such as "whitesplain, rightsplain, gaysplain, journosplain, and straightsplain to one-offs like potlucksplain and grammarsplain" (Perlman, 2019, para.15).

MANSPLAINING IN ACADEMIA

While pointing out mansplaining on social media can be a hoot, it gets trickier in academia. Women still have to sidestep misogynistic hurdles in and out of the classroom even though the number of females has out-paced males in postsecondary institutions for years. For example, females accounted for the majority of college and university students in fall 2018, about 11.2 million compared with 8.7 million males (National Center for Education Statistics, 2018). However, the script is flipped when it comes to faculty, with males dominating numbers across the board.

Of course, there is a difference between mansplaining and narcissistic gas bag–like behavior that is so common in any profession, but especially in one like academia. But telling the difference is not always easy to articulate. It's akin to what Justice Potter Stewart wrote in his 1964 Supreme Court *Jacobellis v. Ohio* opinion on obscenity: "I know it when I see it." Our job as educators, after all, is to teach. We have worked long and hard to become experts in our field. We derive satisfaction, if not joy, from sharing

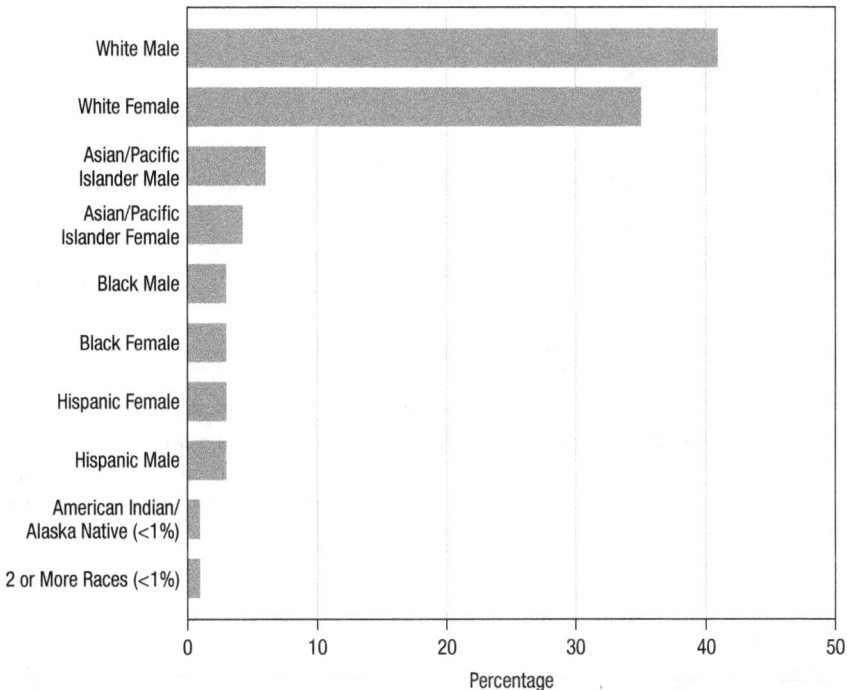

Figure 12.1. Full-time faculty in degree-granting postsecondary institutions, fall 2016.

our knowledge in an effort to help others understand difficult concepts. A line gets crossed, however, when the person doing the explaining is talking to someone who is at least, if not more, of an expert on the subject than he is, according to women academics at various stages of their careers at large, U.S. universities that I communicated with about mansplaining in person, over the phone, and via email.

"Most mansplaining is the result of someone who has self-esteem issues," said one female assistant professor, explaining the difference between mansplaining and straightforward rude behavior. "That's one of the main ingredients in the rude stew as well. I think we see this behavior a lot more in white men these days because there's been a significant political and sociological power shift. I believe white men, those who attend the Church of White Privilege, are feeling threatened by their increasing loss of power and influence."

Another female assistant professor said, "Yes, there is [a difference], though the differences are subtle. While mansplaining takes away a chance at me defending or explaining my work or ideas and views, rude and selfish behavior is also demeaning. Mansplaining and rude behavior are both about power."

A female associate professor said, "I'm not sure it matters. The behavior is unacceptable, and seems to be far more prevalent among men than women."

A female full professor added, "The reasons men do what they do are irrelevant. Putting up with the implication that I don't know as much as they do about anything—large or small—is exhausting, demoralizing, and infuriating, especially at this point in my life. It saps energy that I don't have to waste."

THE IMPACT OF MANSPLAINING

The effect of mansplaining can be one of the many microaggressions women face in postsecondary institutions. A full professor with tenure can stand up to a mansplainer or laugh off an incident more easily than a junior faculty member, needless to say. Junior faculty members can do the same—but they may pay a price. So is mansplaining a minor irritant or something more insidious?

"It's both," said a female full professor. "At the time, it's a minor irritant, but it's actually a symptom of a much larger epidemic, the one in which women *still have* to do more work to get recognized; where we *still* have to shout to be heard in a group of men; where we *still* have to offer proof before we're believed."

A female associate professor said, "It's very serious. It's a micro/macro aggression and can lead to a destructive culture rather than a creative, collaborative one. This is especially true if these aggressions are constant and continuous."

Another female associate professor said, "It's a minor irritant symptomatic of a more serious structural problem of gender inequality."

A female assistant professor said, "This depends on the situation. For example, if someone explains my dissertation work then it's minor. It's my work and I have the degree to prove it. But, say, for example, in a meeting or boardroom, if someone else explains my idea or suggestion, then often the idea or suggestion is attributed to the explainer rather than me who first came up with the stuff."

SHOULD YOU FIGHT MANSPLAINING?

The question, then, is how do you effectively combat mansplaining? How do you encourage everyone, not just women, to point it out when they see it and to check themselves before they do it? Do you call it out yourself? Does doing so depend on your relative position to the mansplainer? Do you choose your battles or ignore all of them out of fear of being pegged an overly sensitive, angry, feminist who can't stand the pressure?

"Early in my career, I silently rolled my eyes to myself and took it [mansplaining]," said a female full professor. "Now I tend to hold up my hands and simply ask them to stop mansplaining and just answer me!"

A female associate professor said, "I find it intensely irritating. I've worked hard to reach my position, and I won't underplay or make a joke about sexist challenges to my authority. When I feel students, TAs, or colleagues are doing so, I'm firm and direct about pushing back."

Another female associate professor said, "I've had to let it go pretty much all of the time. Sometimes it has been my boss or superior mansplaining. If you say something, you'll be perceived as difficult to work with or a complainer. I prove what I know by what I do and eventually hope people will see that."

A female assistant professor said, "I don't call out men for mansplaining nor do I call out people for their rude behavior. It's just too much time and effort and I would rather focus on my work."

What *should* students and faculty do in the face of mansplaining?

"I tell [students] to call guys on it! We can't break this cycle if women don't start 'splaining' back how insulting this approach is," said a female full professor. "Same goes for faculty. Very calmly indicate that you don't need to be 'splained' to and ask to have a convo rather than them giving you a lesson you didn't ask for.'

A female associate professor said, "I would turn this question on its head and ask why the focus on female students. All students should be aware of this and call it out when they see it, preferably in a calm but firm tone. Men can be upstanders. It shouldn't fall only on female faculty members."

A female assistant professor said, "In an ideal world [students and faculty] should stand up for themselves, but it is really up to the leaders of the organization to create a culture where mansplaining is not acceptable."

Another female assistant professor said, "I would like to get proper training in how to deal with this. Like we have orientation, I want to sit down and learn techniques. I want to discuss concerns and learn ways to deal with the fallouts. And I think this will make me a better teacher and educator because an important aspect of my job is to prepare students for the professional world."

WARNING: REACTIONS WILL VARY

Does someone's reaction to mansplaining depend on their "seniority" or "position"?

"It has, but it shouldn't," said a female full professor. "I think my younger female colleagues are really brave and are calling men on it way earlier than I did. I felt I had to get to a certain rank before I could call someone out on it."

Another female full professor said, "I once humorously called out a male junior faculty member for some egregious mansplaining he did in front of students. I was being kind, I thought. I could have really let him have it. Later, he angrily confronted me about it, saying I was out of line and that he was humiliated. So you never know how men will react, no matter how gently you present it. Be prepared for that."

A female associate professor said, "It shouldn't, but it does. People with less authority may need to soften their message with humor or other niceties."

A female assistant professor said, "Yes, it does because power dynamics come into play in every relationship. Also, it's a matter of culture. Some cultures train us not to talk back to older people or be respectful to the point of self-harm. Also, it is a matter of personality and what I am dealing with at the moment. If I just want to leave, I will leave. If I do not want to aggravate my anxiety, I will leave."

MANSPLAINING, MINORITY WOMEN, AND STANDING UP FOR OTHERS

The question of culture is an important one that should not be ignored. Any woman who calls out a mansplainer, no matter what her rank, faces a litany of damaging labels, such as "man-hater" or "difficult." This challenge is amplified for women in the academy who do not identify as cisgender white women because the underlying message in the academy is that we must "know our place" and be "grateful" for what we have lest we also get pegged as the "angry Black woman," the "fiery Latina," or "the Dragon Lady."

As if watching every step and swallowing many slights isn't stressful enough, research shows that minority women often are burdened with extra internal committee work, emotional labor from students, and public demands from panels and interviews at work (Moore, 2017). Citing the work of many other scholars, Moore describes many roadblocks, including added student mentoring, service and advising activities that are not rewarded in department evaluations; less respect for their research; a lack of knowledge about the unwritten rules of university life; a lack of career support and mentors; and a cold institutional climate, especially at primarily white institutions.

For these and other reasons, serious thought should be given to introducing mansplaining to students. Any university program worth its salt, especially one educating students about media, advertising, communications, journalism, public relations, and the like, should be seamlessly weaving content and lessons about diversity, inclusion, and our nation's underserved communities into its curricula so that everyone has some understanding of what people other than ourselves face on a daily basis. Given how regularly a particularly egregious example of mansplaining seems to blow up on social media, it would be easy enough to use it as a discussion or case study in class when discussing gender. Now that you understand what mansplaining is, where the term originated, and why it can be so damaging, below are some strategies to reduce, if not eliminate, mansplaining in the classroom and in the academic workplace.

SUGGESTED ACTIVITIES

1. Introduce the Maynard Institute's Fault Lines approach that teaches reporters to examine five forces that shape lives and social tensions in the United States: race, class, gender, generation, and geography. Ask students to discuss whether there are any other "new" fault lines that could be added to the list. Discuss the intersection of two or more fault lines. https://www.spj.org/dtb2.asp.

2. Choose a local, state, national, or international news source and examine coverage of a major news story. Analyze whether there are instances of men commenting on issues that affect mostly or only women. Discuss whether there are instances of mansplaining or not. Note the inverse, that is, the number of women commenting on issues that affect mostly or only men.

3. Examine social media activity, such as Twitter, around an issue involving women and analyze whether any mansplaining is taking place and/or to what extent it is taking place. Does the Twittersphere point out the mansplaining? If so, what is the general reaction?

4. Conduct a self-audit for a week, month, quarter, or semester and note every time you experience an instance of mansplaining inside or outside the classroom. What was the issue about? How did you respond, if at all? If you responded, how did the person who mansplained react?

5. Conduct role playing exercises in the classroom. Have one person mansplain to another person to practice how to react. Change roles—make it a student-to-student interaction, a professor-to-student interaction, a student-to-professor interaction, and a professor-to-professor interaction. Be sure to practice with a mansplainer reacting angrily to being called out. Practice being an upstander who intervenes, too.

6. If you are an underrepresented minority, especially one attending or working at a primarily white institution, all of the activities

described above can be completed by substituting the term "mansplaining" with the term "whitesplaining," where white people consciously or not speak condescendingly to people of color.

The bottom line is that there is hope. Find allies. Stand up for yourself when it is safe to do so. If you are in a position to support others, by all means, step up. I hope you find this conversation—and these classroom tips—useful. The more we raise awareness about the condescending practice of mansplaining, the better chance there is of ending it once and for all.

REFERENCES

Altma, D. (2018, February 11). Guy tries to mansplain vaginas to women and gynecologists on Twitter, gets annihilated. *Woke Sloth*. Retrieved from https://wokesloth.com/guy-mansplains-vaginas-to-women-and-gynecologists-2/jessi/.

Chen, T. (2019, March 12). A person has been corrected after claiming women only use 7 tampons a period cycle and they should stop "whining" about the costs. BuzzFeed. Retrieved from https://www.buzzfeednews.com/article/tanyachen/a-person-has-been-corrected-after-claiming-women-only-use-7?utm_source=dynamic&utm_campaign=bffbbuzzfeed&ref=bffbbuzzfeed.

Ha, T. (2018, February 25). Dictionary-makers found the first known use of "mansplain." *Quartz*. Retrieved from https://qz.com/1214707/where-does-the-word-mansplain-come-from/.

Lewis, H. (2014, July 4). The essay that launched the term "mansplaining." *The New Republic*. Retrieved from https://newrepublic.com/article/118555/rebecca-solnits-men-explain-things-me-scourge-mansplaining.

Moore, M. R. (2017). Women of color in the academy: Navigating multiple intersections and multiple hierarchies. *Social Problems, 64*(2), 200–205. Retrieved from https://academic.oup.com/socpro/article/64/2/200/3231961.

Murray, D. (2017, May 19). This woman asked Twitter for examples of mansplaining, and boy, did it deliver! *Elle*. Retrieved from https://www.elle.com/uk/life-and-culture/culture/news/a35863/woman-asks-twitter-explanation-mansplaining/.

National Center for Education Statistics, Fast Facts. (2018). *Back to school statistics*. Retrieved from https://nces.ed.gov/fastfacts/display.asp?id=372.

Pandey, S. (2019, May 3). "Mansplain," "OK," "genderqueer," now included in Scrabble dictionary. *Yahoo News*. Retrieved from https://in.news.yahoo.com/mansplain-ok-genderqueer-now-included-151825817.html.

Perlman, M. (2019, February 18). Mansplaining and its offspring. *Columbia Journalism Review*. Retrieved from https://www.cjr.org/language_corner/mansplaining.php.

Solnit, R. (2014). *Men explain things to me*. Chicago, IL: Haymarket Books.

Wilhelm, H. (2017, December). Mansplaining and the gender wars: When argument becomes a weapon. Commentarymagazine.com. Retrieved from https://www.commentarymagazine.com/articles/mansplaining-gender-wars/

13

🌀

Graduate Student Instructors

Tackling Tough Topics for the First Time

Khadija Ejaz

I was asked to write this chapter as a woman of color in academia. Therein lies my dilemma.

I've lived in the United States for two decades, but I am originally from India and grew up in the Middle East, and I don't see myself as "of color." This, though, doesn't stop people in the United States from treating me as if I have a "color." That has had consequences for me in the past. Some were casual, such as not being smiled at or approached for friendships and even relationships, and some were more hostile. Over the years, I have come to realize that people may perceive other things about me—imagined or otherwise—such as gender, age, and sexual orientation. Not having control over how people perceive me upsets me, but knowing that I can't escape the consequences haunts me.

I worried about these things when I was handed my first teaching assignment as a doctoral student. I was in my second year, and while I was very excited, I was concerned about how a class full of mostly Caucasian-origin students from the Deep South would respond to me. The Trump presidential campaign kicked off at the same time, polarizing the U.S. public based on the intersections that had proved challenging to me in the United States. And I taught journalism and research, both topics that were directly under attack by the Trump administration. It made me feel frightened of standing in front of the class, vulnerable and unwelcome, as if I were facing a firing squad.

This chapter highlights the teaching experiences of graduate students like me. This is an important topic because the graduate student body is increasingly looking less like the upper-class European man for whom higher education was designed. According to the Council of Graduate Schools (CGS), as recently as fall 2017, women outnumbered men in both master's and doctoral programs, and underrepresented minorities made up almost a quarter of all first-time graduate program enrollees who were U.S. citizens and permanent residents (CGS, 2018a). Graduate and professional programs are also seeing increasing numbers of students from low-income backgrounds (CGS, 2018b). Moreover, one out of every five graduate students is international (CGS, 2017), numbers that are expected to hold in the future (CGS, 2019). This reality crashes against the entrenched structure of academia. On the one-hundred-year anniversary of women's suffrage in the United States, this chapter seeks to give voice to graduate instructors as they navigate difficult conversations in the classrooms once again.

ENTERING ACADEMIA

In the United States, I am a minority in several ways. I am not white or male or even American. While I am not religious, I am culturally Muslim.

I normally do not think about what I look like to others and whether I have to protect myself from malice or ignorance, but it was on my mind most of the time as a doctoral student and an instructor. I was studying in South Carolina, where Confederate flags are a common sight and where the government observes Confederate Memorial Day. I've seen the Ku Klux Klan protesting the taking down of the Confederate flag from the State House after the Charleston church shooting; the shooter, in fact, was from my area. The names of segregationists adorn buildings and streets, including the Strom Thurmond Wellness and Fitness Center on my campus where I would go swimming. (Thurmond was known for a fiery speech where he used a derogatory word for Black people to say that they would never be allowed in the swimming pools of white people.) The limited public condemnation in South Carolina during the 2016 campaign and beyond made me feel unsafe and paranoid. All this was in addition to the debilitating pressures of being a doctoral student.

I corresponded with several communication graduate students in the United States, and many of them also expressed a similar awareness along various intersections—gender, race, age, language, disability, religion, national origin. Noella[1] is a doctoral student who migrated to the United States from Mexico as a child, and according to her, there are two versions

---

1. Acknowledging the vulnerable positions of graduate students and the sensitive nature of the topic, I have assigned the participants pseudonyms and withheld other identifiable pieces of information from their interviews.

of graduate school, one that is experienced by white people and another that is experienced by everyone else. In this way, academia reminds Eleanor of the rest of the world. A Black woman, she spent many years in broadcast journalism and is now a doctoral student. "I still feel as if academia (overall) is a space that is not structured for women and students of color," she said. "It was essentially created for white men." Nicole, also a Black doctoral student, recounted similar feelings about her university, whose climate she called "hostile, elitist, sexist, racist, and classist."

> There have been white supremacist rallies on campus, frequent Neo-Nazi symbols on campus, two overt racist incidents against the university Black community (a Blackface incident and a sorority member saying a racial slur), an increased number of rapes on campus, and the university was ranked third in universities not friendly to the LGBTQI+ community; and all the university does is provide lip service statements about diversity and inclusion when these issues occur. It feels like *all* underrepresented students in general are not appreciated and are only here to fulfill a quota.

By now, Nicole feels tired, disappointed, and disengaged by this atmosphere. "The political climate at the university has worn me down to the point I am starting not to care," she confessed. According to her, the lack of an appropriate reaction from her university makes underrepresented students feel unsafe, unimportant, and discouraged. I heard concerns about not being perceived as credible. "I wish I had known that when you walk into a room as a short, brown woman, people will question your authority," said Tahira, a doctoral student of mixed Arab and Spanish origin who grew up in an immigrant family in the Deep South. Ofra is an Arab Muslim woman and a doctoral student from the Middle East, and she describes being underrepresented as always feeling pressured to stay true to oneself.

> Sometimes it means that you put extra effort not only to prove yourself but first erase what preconceived ideas the majority have of you. In both cases, you, the whole package of you—your ideas, your beliefs and values—are always perceived as less, less important, less relevant, less serious.

ENTERING THE CLASSROOM

These challenges followed the graduate students as they began to teach undergraduate students. Many of them reported being treated with disrespect by their students in various ways. Nicole felt that students behaved this way because they were empowered and protected by universities.

Grades appeared to be one of the topics of pushback. Lydia, a white female doctoral student, had a student complain about her to the dean of her school, and Noella once had a student become so confrontational that the instructor of record had to intervene.

One source of difficulty appeared to be the gender of the graduate students. Nieve is a doctoral student from Puerto Rico, and according to her, students are generally more likely to respect and comply with male instructors than with female instructors. "In other words," she said, "male instructors are perceived as tough, whereas female instructors are perceived as bitches." Nicole was referred to in student evaluations as "girl" instead of by her name.

This dynamic also appeared to dovetail with race. In Lydia's case, her gender and the topics she was teaching—racism, sexism, homophobia, and Islamophobia in the media—appeared to influence how her students behaved with her.

> While many of the students commented that our in-class discussions really opened their eyes to things they had never thought about, others specifically commented that I was a liberal feminist trying to push my thoughts/opinions onto them. The minorities in the class would regularly send me emails thanking me for creating a space where we could have these discussions and for being excited to start the conversation.

The current political climate seemed to influence the pushback that graduate student instructors received from their students, particularly those who were white. This resistance often occurred with graduate student instructors who weren't white. Both Noella and Nicole described receiving silence from their white students on topics related to diversity, inclusion, and marginalization. Noella felt that the current political climate had encouraged her students to make comments that were insensitive and borderline racist.

> For example, in one of the classes that I taught, my students were talking about immigration, and they were talking about the terms "illegal" and "undocumented." They specifically mentioned that "illegal" and "undocumented" were the same terms, only with different connotations. On campus there are over 500 undocumented students, some of which are in the communication department. The term "illegal" is a derogatory term, which—in my experience—has been used more frequently under the Trump regime. So, as an underrepresented graduate student instructor, I had to be able to navigate these conversations in a way that I wouldn't be seen as a token instructor, which made teaching harder.

Noella also described receiving pushback with the concepts she would teach her students, something that the white members of her cohort did not experience. Nicole, too, had similar experiences. She faced a disruptive white student in a class she cotaught with an international graduate student; her student would cut the instructors off during discussions and was rude to the other instructor during office hours.

At the end of the day, the graduate students wished they had more support from administrators. This lack of oversight is what surprised Lydia more at the end of her two years of teaching as a doctoral student:

> No one is looking at our course evaluations, no one is sitting in on our classes to give us feedback, no one is even looking at the syllabus to make sure we're teaching what should be taught. Shouldn't there be some level of coaching and oversight for graduate students? I think if I had known that we would be "thrown to the wolves," I would've asked more questions going into my first semester of teaching or maybe asked for feedback throughout the semester.

MEETING AT INTERSECTIONS

During my conversations with the graduate students, I was happy to see them bring up the idea of intersections. It is something I have learned to think about in my own life inside and outside the classroom. I first heard about this concept as a doctoral student, and it made me realize that there are ways in which I have privilege, such as being heterosexual and cisgendered. I try to remember that whenever I feel too negative. It is a useful reminder that I do have a certain amount of power and privilege that I can use not only for myself but for others. Danielle is a doctoral student, and she echoed my sentiments, emphasizing her privileges as a white, cisgender, and able-bodied person. "I think it's important to remember and continuously evaluate how the privileges of that positionality, particularly as white, can both marginalize and shed light on others who must fight against further underrepresentation," she said.

The graduate students I spoke to also often spoke about harnessing the power of their underrepresented intersections. It reminded me of some advice I had received from a supervisor in my department before teaching my first-ever course. He had told me that the best thing I could do for my students was to be my whole multicultural self while teaching because, at my predominantly white institution, that would probably be the most exposure most of my students would get in their lives. Ofra has learned to see her difference as an opportunity, a difference that can allow her to explore understudied areas. "Students and professors will look forward to working with you when they need input in those fields," she said. According to Tahira, she spent her life navigating being both an American and a woman of color, and like Ofra, she feels that she is able to use her unique position as an instructor:

I am able to effectively communicate about issues regarding Islamophobia and racism with my students who come from white, middle-class backgrounds because that is exactly who I grew up around. Students feel comfortable coming to me with their questions because even though I am a woman of color, they know I will meet them where they are without judging them.

ACTIVITIES

1. List out the various intersections in your identity.

   a) Which intersections bring you privilege?
   b) What can you do with that privilege?
   c) Which intersections take privilege away from you?
   d) For each intersection in c), identify three people, places, or things that can give you support.

2. Ask your students to list out the various intersections in their identities.

   a) Which intersections take privilege away from them?
   b) For the intersections in a), ask them to describe instances when they felt minimized or marginalized.
   c) Which intersections bring them privilege?
   d) What can they do with that privilege?

3. Give your students more insight into what you do. On the first day of class, tell them about all your responsibilities as a graduate student and where you fit into the scheme of things in the department and academia. Tell them why you are in graduate school and what your life will look like once you graduate.

4. Give your students more insight into the evaluation process. Tell them what it is for. At the same time, make them aware that some instructors are treated better than others. For example, inform them of research that says that male instructors are evaluated less harshly than female instructors and that some in academia consider evaluations discriminatory.

5. Bring up difficult topics in class. Ask your students to apply the concepts they learn in class to real-life events.

6. Introduce diversity in your teaching material. Nicole is conscious about the visuals she includes when she teaches. She specifically tries to use pictures and videos of diverse people. I have done the same while designing questions for my exams; I try to include characters and situations in my questions that represent a wide variety of people and cultures.

7. Download the American Psychological Association of Graduate Students (APAGS) Resource Guide for Ethnic Minority Graduate Students from https://www.apa.org/apags/resources/ethnic-minority-guide/. This free publication includes general information for underrepresented graduate students both for school and beyond. It also addresses specific issues that such students may face, like racism, lack of mentors, and imposter syndrome.

According to Eleanor, "each person has a superpower with being who they are," and the unique insights gained from one's underrepresented identities has many benefits. First, instructors are able to understand their underrepresented students better. "I can identify with the new international student who feels out of place and sits quietly in the classroom for fear of saying something culturally insensitive," said Nieve.

Second, these insights can fuel one's lessons. The graduate students I spoke to encouraged using personal stories to enhance one's lessons. Eleanor is open with her students about the challenges she faces as a Black person, mother, and woman. "I also share with them reasons why I want to be a professor, which was to be the professor I never had." Her students respond well to her openness, describing her as a "breath of fresh air," being the first Black instructor for many of them even as far as into their third year. Lydia too has shared her struggles as a white woman with two adopted Hispanic daughters:

> For example, when we were discussing institutionalized racism in my class this semester, I admitted that as a white female I had never experienced racism until I enrolled my Hispanic daughters into public school. I shared stories of how the teachers treated my daughters differently after they realized their parents were white and about how the school system failed my girls when we reported racist bullying. While I had never personally experienced racism, the feedback I received from the students was positive, so I'd highly recommend to others that they share as much about their personal identities and experiences as possible to show others what it's like outside of the world they know.

Nicole uses this approach to teach students how one's positionality can affect one's construction of stories and how one gathers information. She specifically talks about purposefully finding diverse sources to provide multiple perspectives on an issue. Danielle teaches her journalism students about the policymaking mantra "nothing about us without us," encouraging them to interview a diverse array of sources beyond the usual politician and professor. According to Noella, this can help students appreciate the process of knowledge production and especially make students of color feel that their experiences have a place in higher education.

Morrison is a Black female doctoral student, and she likes to purposely inject current issues affecting marginalized populations into class discussions. "Being in the South, I realized that some students' points of view would clash," she said, "so I consciously listened (read) points of view and allowed the text with factual information support." Morrison found that most of her students responded well to this technique. They appreciated the new knowledge and were eager to learn. Tahira's experiences as an instructor have not always been as smooth; she shares one such turbulent experience and how she handled it:

In one of my lectures on Islamophobia, one student called me an anti-Semite (though I made no mention of Jews), and another claimed that their religion (Christianity) was being attacked, though I made no anti-Christian remarks. In fact, I am Christian myself. However, while there will always be a share of challenging students, you can be sure that you'll have some "woke" ones too. During the lecture, if a student disagreed or challenged something I said, another student would respond. This is exactly what I want to happen in the classroom. I want to facilitate discussion and allow the students to cultivate their critical thinking skills. I am not afraid of being challenged. I encourage it. Also, I saw what didn't work in my Islamophobia lecture that year and adjusted. Every group of students is different. You have to meet them where they are.

GOING FORWARD

The advice in the previous section represents what graduate student instructors can do to ease their challenges in the classroom in the short run. They also offered their thoughts on more long-term solutions to the problems faced by graduate student instructors, especially those who are underrepresented in academia.

What Institutions Can Do

The role of the institution emerges as crucial in the discussions in this chapter. One of the suggestions I gleaned from my conversations was to offer cultural training to faculty, staff, and graduate students. Emma, a white doctoral student, believes that this is an area that is often overlooked because of lack of time and awareness, even when such training is available.

> Training addresses those who are already on the payroll. Similar changes can also be achieved by hiring a diverse array of people, including those with diverse identities as well as diverse areas of expertise. Departments can also arrange for diverse guest speakers.

According to Eleanor, "it should be more than just checking a box or for a quota." At the same time, universities should acknowledge the larger share of service responsibilities that fall to underrepresented faculty. Noella suggests counting their mentorship as part of service and not discounting their research if it emerges from their identities and personal experiences.

Institutions should also do more to care for their graduate students who may face additional pressure to be a great example. Nicole suggests listening to underrepresented students, including understanding how the institution itself may be part of the problem. Acknowledging the heritage and culture of the underrepresented students is another approach. "Try to know one or two major events in their countries or religious beliefs," Ofra said. "Send them an email, wish them happy Eid / Ramadan / National day when you see them. It does make a lot of difference."

What Graduate Students Can Do

Mentorship and the need for a support group emerged often in my conversations with graduate student instructors. Noella felt secure knowing that her instructors of record have supported her in the past, even in disputes with students. These do not need to be limited to one's own department. Morrison said that she had found a network of African Americans in her campus community who "assist in keeping sanity and provide a space for venting and strategizing to survive." Even other graduate students can be a source of support.

Ultimately, the graduate students I talked to expressed the need to protect themselves. Nicole credits her institution's conservative and Confederate ties to being told to be careful about what she talks about in her classes and to speak in a certain way. Morrison recommends being strategic in one's approach, like prioritizing one's studies over other responsibilities, like teaching, and to document anything that goes amiss.

> I learned that I can't prevent folks from seeing me as an incompetent, out-of-place Black girl. And carrying that burden affected my health in the past. I harness a magical power from the margins, where I seek to influence more than battling constantly. It's not easy because we have expectations of the same treatment as our white counterparts. Realistically, that will never happen. So using your voice strategically and understanding the political environment helps.

CONCLUSION

"I have spent the last five years of my life constantly feeling out of place, like I do not truly belong anywhere. My only validation at times is when people share stories like mine. I always find comfort in these moments: we are not alone" (Guzmán, 2019, p. 338).

The quote above is from a paper by Lynette DeAun Guzmán. Guzmán was a graduate student in mathematics education who graduated in 2017, and in her paper, she describes how she felt as a Latinx woman navigating academia with the zeitgeist of the 2016 election campaign. I discovered her paper, "Academia Will Not Save You: Stories of Being Continually Underrepresented," while putting this chapter together. I wrote this chapter while transitioning into my first faculty position, and the words of the graduate students in this chapter as well as those of Guzmán made me feel like I may be wanted in academia after all. I didn't always feel that way as a doctoral student. As I close this chapter, I encourage you to use Guzmán's paper as a conversation starter both in and out of the classroom. You may be relieved by where it takes you.

REFERENCES

Council of Graduate Schools. (2017). 2017 Reports. Retrieved from https://cgsnet .org/2017-reports.

Council of Graduate Schools. (2018a, October 3). First-time enrollment holds steady, Application counts slightly decline at U.S. graduate schools. Retrieved from https://cgsnet.org/first-time-enrollment-holds-steady-application -counts-slightly-decline-us-graduate-schools.

Council of Graduate Schools. (2018b). 2018 Reports. Retrieved from https://cgs net.org/2018-reports.

Council of Graduate Schools. (2019, February 7). International graduate applications and enrollments continue to decline at U.S. institutions. Retrieved from https://cgsnet.org/international-graduate-applications-and-enrollments-con tinue-decline-us-institutions.

Flaherty, C. (2019, June 13). When white scholars pick white scholars. *Inside Higher Ed*. Retrieved from https://www.insidehighered.com/news/2019/06/13/ communication-scholars-debate-how-fields-distinguished-scholars-should -be-picked?fbclid=IwAR2KjqjhCi7ISXUhczJHmL-WkCgjCpAXdH4Vzxw BUaav8QItaE_wA5LVT_U.

Guzmán, L. D. (2019). Academia will not save you: Stories of being continually "underrepresented." *Journal of Humanistic Mathematics, 9*(1), 326–343.

McCourtney Institute for Democracy. (n.d.). CDD statement on controversy in the national communication association. Pennsylvania State University. Retrieved from https://democracy.psu.edu/nca.

14

An Intersectional LGBTQ+ Pop Culture Approach to Critical Pedagogy

Nathian Shae Rodriguez

This chapter utilizes autoethnography, focusing on my phenomeno-logical experiences and pedagogical practices, to evidence how using mediated examples can foster intersectionality in the classroom. The goal of the chapter is to provide critical pedagogy (CP) that can be employed across all courses in a media and communication university curriculum. CP is both a philosophic and pedagogical paradigm first introduced by Paulo Freire in his book *Pedagogy of the Oppressed* (1970) and further con-ceptualized in *Pedagogy of Hope* (1992) and *Pedagogy of Freedom* (1998). The concept of a critical pedagogy is rooted in a sense of urgency and activism through teaching that is relevant, reflexive, and critically informed. CP has been employed by instructors across a range of disciplines to teach issues of diversity, equity, inclusion, and social justice in college and uni-versity courses. Issues of identity, such as race/ethnicity, gender, sexual orientation, religion, and other identity markers are germane to critical pedagogy. Identities, however, are not monolithic but rather intersec-tional. Therefore, the pedagogical approaches in educational spaces must also be intersectional.

Like all educational spaces, media and communication spaces shape and maintain critical dialogue, fostering knowledge through creation and sharing. CP can be applied in these courses, specifically, to cultivate identity-based awareness and, in some instances, activism. I argue that general communication courses are not as inclusive of identities that are considered marginalized. Basic communication courses most often sym-bolically annihilate these identities. Instructors or institutions may deem

LGBTQ, and sometimes race/ethnicity and gender, content as controversial or not relevant to "mainstream" communication topics. Some instructors may not feel qualified to speak on certain identity issues because their own personal intersection of identities does not include specific marginalized identities. Therefore, this chapter will aid in setting forth an agenda to specifically highlight intersectional LGBTQ identities and their intersections by employing CP with an intersectional lens. First, I will provide a brief overview of critical pedagogy and intersectionality. Using this theoretical nexus, I will provide critical and discursive pedagogical strategies that I have used in my classroom that can be used in media and communication courses to integrate intersectional content.

FROM CRITICAL PEDAGOGY TO POP CULTURE PEDAGOGY

Paulo Freire's (1970) conceptualization of CP is rooted in critical theory and was informed by Freire's lived experiences "in poverty stricken northeastern Brazil in the 1960s." Kincheloe (2007) wrote that "critical pedagogy amalgamated liberation theological ethics and the critical theory of the Frankfurt School in Germany with the progressive impulses in education" (p. 12). Freire (1970) believed that individuals, specifically students, should question ideologies and practices they consider oppressive and work both as individuals and collectives to respond to those oppressive conditions in their own lives. CP posits that individuals are able to construct a critical view of the world through a process of dialogue with others. Through a critical dialogic exchange, individuals are made aware of their interconnectedness and their responsibility to others. Educational spaces provide opportunities to foster critical dialogue, resulting in knowledge creation and sharing. These opportunities are interdependent, involving both instructor and student.

The role of the instructor is not to mirror traditional practices of pedagogy that echo oppressive society in educational settings. Rather, the instructor helps facilitate a critical dialogic process with and among students, creating and recreating knowledge. This critical pedagogy results in a critical consciousness that Freire (1970) terms "conscientizacão"— "learning to perceive social, political, and economic contradictions, and to take action against the oppressive elements of reality" (p. 35). Conscientizacão fosters a sense of self-affirmation and purpose in instructors and students. Thus, CP is a transformation-based approach that enables individuals to question and respond to oppressive practices and ideologies.

I argue that the same agenda, beliefs, and goals are able to be applied to media and communication courses in a broad and general sense in the form of critical and intersectional pop culture pedagogy. Specifically, the tenets of CP can be applied to "make relevant" intersectional identities, specifically rooted in and around LGBTQ identities and better comprehend the role of communication as "constitutive (and, thus, constraining) of our understandings and relationships" (Friere, 1970, p. 5).

INTERSECTIONALITY

Identity in and of itself is not monolithic, but rather made up of various identities that intersect and overlap. Kimberlé Crenshaw (1990) conceptualized this intersection of identities as intersectionality. She posits that these intersections not only intersect, but interact to create lived experiences for each individual that are qualitatively different from another. These intersections both privilege and oppress individuals, depending on the identities. Crenshaw first illustrated this concept using race and gender, arguing that the two identity categories were not mutually exclusive. She evidenced her argument with Black women, highlighting their lived experiences as subordinated. For example, Crenshaw pointed out that Black women often have less access to economic, social, and political gains and are disproportionately subjected to violence. Intersectionality was later expanded to other minorities through various lines of research. Thus, multiple forms of discrimination (sexism and racism in her original conceptualization, for example) intersect, overlap, and sometimes combine in the lived experiences of marginalized individuals to create multiple levels of social injustice.

Crenshaw (1990) further explicated intersectionality into three categories: structural, political, and representational. Structural intersectionality is the location of specific identities an individual possesses that makes their actual lived experiences qualitatively different than other individuals. In the case of Black women, Crenshaw gave the examples of poverty, child care, lack of job skills, cultural barriers, gender discrimination, and class oppression, among others. Political intersectionality describes how conflicting political agendas may exist for intersecting identities. For example, women's rights movements may focus on women, but neglect women of color. Black rights movements may focus on Black individuals, but more so on Black men and less on Black women. Thus a Black woman is twice marginalized in these political movements. Representational intersectionality speaks to the cultural construction of intersectional identities and how those intersections are represented in cultural imagery, such as media.

Since Crenshaw's (1990) original conceptualization, *intersectionality* has been expanded to include other marginalized identities and continues to be a site of resistance for subordinated groups, including those identifying along the LGBTQ continuum. One criticism of modern research, however, has been its use as an umbrella term to describe an individual's multitude of identities. In a 2017 interview with MSNBC, Crenshaw reiterated that the concept can be used for multiple marginalized groups (specifically addressing LGBTQ identities) and warned against using it as a blanket term or grand theory of everything. Her intention, she argues, is that intersectionality "is a lens through which you can see where power comes and collides, where it interlocks and intersects" (Columbia, 2017, para. 4). Intersectionality shines a light on these issues of multiple oppressions and allows for better intervention in advocacy.

Thus, this chapter asks what critical and discursive pedagogical strategies can be used in media and communication courses to integrate intersectional content.

AUTOETHNOGRAPHY IN MEDIA AND SEXUALITY

I employed an analytic autoethnography as the methodology to collect pedagogical data. Anderson (2006) outlines five key criteria that a researcher must meet in order to conduct an analytic autoethnography. The researcher must be a full member of the group and setting being studied; practice analytical reflexivity; maintain narrative visibility of the researcher's self by serving as the primary subject of the story; engage with dialogue with informants beyond themselves; and be committed to developing a broader theoretical understanding. From this five-point perspective I was better able to understand my positionality in relation to the research setting and the larger autoethnographic project.

I utilized upper-level university courses centered on media and communication that I taught as the instructor of record. The autoethnography was conducted over the course of two academic years, 2018 and 2019, encompassing three semesters with three different groups of students. Throughout the observation and data collection process, I practiced systematic sociological introspection, emotional recall, as well as reflected on cognitions, emotions, and physical sensations of both myself and my students. Successful critical communication pedagogical practices that used intersectional pop culture–mediated content of LGBTQ individuals was compiled into four main strategic areas of content: real-world examples, streaming media shows and movies, music videos, and podcasts.

Strategy 1: Integrating Real-World Examples in Real Time with Mediated Texts

Current events in politics and pop culture provide timely and relevant backdrops for lectures and class discussions. During the two years of observation, I was able to use many of these events in the course to highlight instances of LGBTQ issues that directly related back to topics being covered in the course. For example, International Women's Day, the Women's March, and various religious freedom bills were some political events I used. Also, the Trump regime made decisions that directly impacted LGBTQ individuals, such as rescinding bathroom protections for transgender students, banning people from Muslim nations, and directing hateful rhetoric toward Mexicans and migrants (many who fled due to persecution for their sexual orientation).

In regards to pop culture, the Academy Awards, the #MeToo movement, Pride month (including advertising and corporate social responsibility), Super Bowl advertisements, and celebrity coming out moments were also used across my courses. Whether political or pop culture, real-world examples in real time were used to highlight topics that students were already talking about outside the classrooms, many of which directly impacted the identities of the students. I was able to pair media coverage and live footage of the event with theory and praxis. This provided students with a more holistic view of mediated effects.

One real-life event that I have employed repeatedly in my classes is that of Jussie Smollett, an openly gay Black actor. Smollett was the star of the FOX television series *Empire*, where his character was also an openly gay Black musician. In January 2019, Smollett filed a police report saying he was attacked in Chicago by two men who beat him and called him racial and homophobic slurs. A month later, Smollett was indicted for disorderly conduct for staging a fake attack and filing a false police report. Two months later, in March 2019, all charges against Smollett were dropped. The public used social media to both support and condemn Smollett.

I use this event to highlight the intersectional identities of sexual orientation, race/ethnicity, gender, and hip-hop. I show my class episodes from *Empire* and supplement them with academic readings on quare theory, mascing, and masculinity. Included in the readings is a study I conducted that evidences how *Empire* reifies queer stereotypes, while underscoring conventions of Black masculinity and hip-hop authenticity (Rodriguez, 2018b). Students discuss the episodes and Smollett's characters in small groups and then compare and contrast their findings with other mediated queer characters. The following class period, we view media coverage of Smollett's attack, indictment, and the dropping of his charges. We also view social media posts of support and condemnation, as well as various press conferences and interviews that Smollett participated in. I ask the students to compare and contrast the coverage between various media outlets and how Smollett's intersectional identity influences the media coverage.

In two class periods, students are exposed to various facets of media and communication methods, theories, and areas, using Smollett as a focal point. This not only helps foster their use of pragmatic examples to explain the academic literature they are reading, but it also helps them better understand the systemic intersectional oppressions that are intrinsically tied to particular identities and the media's role in reinforcing or challenging those oppressions.

Strategy 2: Integrating Streaming Media Shows and Movies

Streaming media platforms are not only more inclusive of marginalized identities, but are arguably more intersectional than network, cable, and premium channels (Rodriguez, 2018b). Streaming shows and movies on digital media platforms such as Netflix, Hulu, Amazon Prime, and YouTube can be integrated into your courses to highlight characters and plotlines that revolve around LGBTQ intersectional identities. The platforms are easily accessible on mobile devices, laptops, and in-classroom computers. There is, however, an issue of subscription when considering assigning at-home viewing.

Streaming media shows with intersectional characters and context include *Queer Eye, One Day at a Time, The Fosters, Orange Is the New Black, The Unbreakable Kimmy Schmidt, Sex Education, Special, Black Lightning, Casa de Flores, Élite, Sense8, Pose,* and *Styling Hollywood* on Netflix; *I Am Jazz, Marvel's Runaways, The Bisexual,* and *The Bold Type* on Hulu; *Vida* and *Now Apocalypse* on STARZ Play streaming service; *Euphoria, Six Feet Under, The Wire, Here and Now, Los Espookys,* and *Looking* on HBO Go and HBO Now; and *Brujos* on the web. This list is not exhaustive, but still offers some great shows across a spectrum of streaming platforms that instructors can use in their courses. It is also important to note that some of the shows listed for Netflix and Hulu are not Netflix or Hulu originals, but rather are housed on the platforms for streaming purposes.

Movies with LGBTQ characters are numerous across the streaming platforms; however, movies with intersectional and minority characters are still scarce. GLADD noted that in 2018 there was an uptick in LGBTQ characters in movies overall (18.2 percent); in spite of this, only 42 percent were people of color—a decrease from 57 percent in 2017 (Brown, 2019). The intersectional movies that I assign to my classes for at-home viewing include *Moonlight; To Wong Foo, Thanks for Everything! Julie Newmar; Y Tu Mamá También, Paris Is Burning, Rent, The Bird Cage,* and *Pariah.* These movies have both excellent examples of intersectional characters, as well as very stereotypical examples. All are great visual aids and learning opportunities for students.

YouTube is another great platform to integrate intersectional mediated examples. Josh Leyva's *Gaylo* series and his *Gaylo Returns* movie evidence the use of stereotypes based on cultural identity, geography, sexual orientation, and gender. World of Wonder's YouTube channel WowPresents hosts various intersectional drag queen–centric web series, such as *Fashion Photo Ruview, La Vida de Valentina, I Want to Be a K-Pop Idol with Soju!,* and *Monét's Herstory X Change*. I especially like using the web series from WowPresents because they allow the drag queens to be themselves, have creative control of their performances, and provide intersectional context that is absent from mainstream television. In general, YouTube web-based episodes are usually five to fifteen minutes in length, making them perfect for in-class viewing or quick at-home viewing assignments.

I want to highlight two streaming shows I use in my courses. The first is the Netflix series *Special*. The show centers on a gay man with cerebral palsy and his sexual coming of age. Students watch an episode or two in class (each is about twenty-five minutes long) and then reflect in small groups about the content. I have them think about what counts as disability and who decides, as well as what other images of disability and sexual orientation we see in other mediated texts. I then ask them to consider the role of nondisabled actors/actresses in disabled roles and their implications. I pair this show with literature on crip theory, social construction, cinema of isolation, and a TED Talk on YouTube by Maysoon Zayid titled "I Got 99 Problems . . . Palsy Is Just One."

I also use the Netflix stand-up special *Hannah Gadsby: Nanette*. Gadsby is openly queer and the special focused on her personal experience with gender, sexuality, and childhood trauma. Although it is a stand-up comedy show, Gadsby opens up intimately and there are many emotional moments. I ask students to watch the special and then reflect on how Gadsby's use of medium and delivery is both intersectional and impactful. They deconstruct the show and the use of stand-up as a conduit for social critique and critical thought.

Strategy 3: Integrating Music Videos

Music videos are a great way to exhibit intersectional identities in mediated pop culture and get the attention of students. Musicians and artists use music videos to add visual elements and context to their lyrics and sounds. Music videos often convey the intersectional identities of these musical artists, as well as societal issues that center on marginalization. LGBTQ-specific music videos have increased in recent years; however, intersectional videos are not as numerous. Across my classes, I use music videos at the beginning of classes to increase the energy level of the students and instigate critical thinking.

Videos that I have used to highlight intersectional LGBTQ identities include "Nails, Hair, Hips, Heels" by Todrick Hall; "Insulto" by Francisca Valenzuela; "Nikes" by Frank Ocean; "Ghost" by Halsey; "Girlfriend" by MNEK; "Faint of Heart" by Tegan and Sarah; "PYNK" by Janelle Monáe; "Augustine" by Blood Orange; "New Orleans" by Brockhampton and Jaden Smith; "Flowerbomb" by Siena Liggins; "What I Need" by Hayley Kiyoko and Kehlani; "Pray" by Sam Smith; and

"American Pie" by Shea Diamond. These videos foster critical reflection on the linkages between pop culture and modern society and prompt students to think about how music can be used as a counterhegemonic tool to combat intersectional oppressions.

I use the video "Make Me Feel" by Janelle Monáe to highlight how music can be not only unapologetically queer, but also how, when paired with visuals, it can directly address intersectional issues of gender and race/ethnicity. I have students go over the lyrics first before I show them the video. I have them perform a textual analysis of sorts to find themes of intersectionality and expression. Students then watch the video and discuss how the visuals reinforce or take away from their findings. Students work in groups and discuss the implications for audiences of all identities.

I also show "Caro" by Bad Bunny to showcase issues of masculinity and gender in Latin trap music and Latinx culture. The song's title translates to "expensive" in English and highlights marginalized groups, including LGBTQ and women, in nontraditional gender roles and gender fluidity. For example, it highlights cisgender men getting manicures and painting their nails. The video was inspired by Bad Bunny's own experience in Spain, where a salon refused him service. I ask students to first highlight instances in the video that are indicative of machismo/machista practices in the Latinx culture and how they are mediated through music and music videos. I then ask them to compare and contrast those practices to not only mainstream U.S. culture, but also their own respective cultures and intersectional identities.

"Trash" by Tyler Glenn takes a hard stance against the antigay views of the Church of Jesus Christ of Latter-day Saints. Tyler, former front man of Neon Trees and an ex-Mormon, came out in 2014 and used music to speak out against the church's opposition of same-sex cohabitation and marriage. Although his album *Excommunication* has many intersectional songs, "Trash" in particular has an accompanying video laden with symbols of his identity negotiation. I pair the "Trash" video with a YouTube video from a Radio.com interview where Tyler explains the symbolism in the video. It's a great opportunity for students to engage with theories like symbolic interactionism and social identity, as well as see how religion and LGBTQ identity intersect in pop culture.

Strategy 4: Integrating Podcasts

Podcasts are an excellent way to integrate intersectional media, created by and for intersectional audiences, into your course. Specifically, they evidence how students themselves can make media content using their own intersectional voices (Rodriguez, 2018b). I find they are a great example of both content and process. Podcasts like *Busy Being Black*; *Café Con Chisme*; *Tamarindo*; *Locatora Radio*; *Hoodrat to Headwrap, A Decolonized Podcast*; *The Gay Footballer's Podcast*; *Minority Korner*; *Brothaspeak*; *Magical Boys*; *She Said What!?*; *Still Processing*; and *The Read* are among the few I assign across my courses.

Disability After Dark with Andrew Gurza is a podcast that I like to assign to students to listen to at home in preparation for discussion on identities that intersect with disability. The host is an out and proud disabled gay man who focuses on sex, dating, and ableism. This podcast is usually assigned to students with a reading on crip theory by Robert McRuer called "Disabling Sex: Notes for a Crip Theory of Sexuality." I have the students listen to the podcast and read an article at home. Then when they come to class, they get into groups and discuss the podcast using a crip lens. Gurza, the podcast's creator, also created the viral hashtag #DisabledPeopleAreHot. I have students do an in-class group exercise where they perform a short textual analysis on Twitter using the hashtag and share their findings with the class.

Another intersectional podcast I use in my courses is *Black, Trans, & Beautiful*. The hostess, Yannick Taylor, primarily focuses on her experiences of being Black and trans, usually inviting other Black trans folx on the show. The most recent way I've integrated this podcast into my course is by assigning a podcast episode that centered on the FX show *Pose*. I had students listen to the episode at home and then discuss it in small groups in class. I then had the students look up memes of *Pose*, both positive and negative, and have a critical discussion on how media have traditionally represented trans women of color in comparison to the show *Pose*. Students then employed makeameme.org and imgflip.com to make their own memes using *Pose* characters and using transgender theory as a guide in class.

I also use *Bitter Brown Femmes* as a way to help explain the concept of Latinx to students, as well as evidence on how media can be used as a form of resistance and social justice. The hosts, Cassandra and Rubén, identify as queer Xicanos and focus on topics that intersect media, politics, social justice, and pop culture with Latinx identity. I assign various episodes of the podcast to students and pair it with scenes from Netflix's *One Day at a Time*. Specifically, the scenes I use highlight Elena, who explicitly identifies as Latinx and lesbian, and her use of social justice, gender pronouns, and relationships with her family.

CONCLUSION

Critical pedagogy (CP) can be applied to media and communication courses in a broad and general sense. Specifically, the strategies outlined above will "make relevant" intersectional identities in our students to better comprehend the role of intersectional media in society. More specific, the strategies of implementing real-world examples, streaming media shows and movies, music videos, and podcasts will help instructors facilitate a critical dialogue with and among students. This helps to not only create and re-create knowledge (an outcome of CP), but also fosters a critical consciousness where students will learn how to perceive and take action against social, political, and economic contradictions (Freire, 1970).

Employing a CP approach in media and communication (including but not limited to journalism, advertising, public relations, and media studies) will not only make relevant the teaching and research of our discipline, but it will also validate and incorporate the intersectional facets of identities in both students and instructors. Because CP is a transformation-based approach, it will enable students to question and respond to oppressive practices and ideologies within and beyond the discipline of media and communication.

REFERENCES

Anderson, L. (2006). Analytic autoethnography. *Journal of Contemporary Ethnography, 35*(4), 373–395.

Brown, T. (2019, May 23). GLAAD report: LGBTQ representation in films is up, but less diverse. *The Los Angeles Times.* Retrieved from https://www.latimes.com/entertainment/ movies/ la-et-mn-lgbtq-representation-glaad-studio-responsibility-index-20190523-story.html.

Columbia Law School. (2017, June 8). Kimberlé Crenshaw on intersectionality: More than two decades later. *Columbia Law News.* Retrieved from https://www.law.columbia.edu/ pt-br/ news/ 2017/ 06/ kimberle-crenshaw-intersectionality.

Crenshaw, K. (1990). Mapping the margins: Intersectionality, identity politics, and violence against women of color. *Stanford Law Review, 43*(6), 1241–1299.

Eguchi, S., Calafell, B. M., & Files-Thompson, N. (2014). Intersectionality and quare theory: Fantasizing African American male same-sex relationships in *Noah's Arc: Jumping the Broom. Communication, Culture & Critique, 7*(3), 371–389.

Ellis, C. S., & Bochner, A. (2000). Autoethnography, personal narrative, reflexivity: Researcher as subject. In N. K. Denzin & Y. S. Lincoln (Eds.), *Handbook of qualitative research* (733–768). Thousand Oaks, CA: Sage.

Freire, P. (1970/2003). *Pedagogy of the oppressed: 30th anniversary edition.* New York, NY: Continuum.

Freire, P. (1992). *Pedagogy of hope: Reliving Pedagogy of the Oppressed.* New York, NY: Continuum.

Freire, P. (1998). *Pedagogy of freedom: Ethics, democracy, and civic courage.* Lanham MD: Rowman & Littlefield.

Johnson, E. P. (2001). "Quare" studies, or (almost) everything I know about queer studies I learned from my grandmother. *Text and Performance Quarterly, 21*(1), 1–25.

Kincheloe, J. L. (2007). Critical pedagogy in the twenty-first century: Evolution for survival. In P. McLaren & J. L. Kincheloe (Eds.), *Critical pedagogy: Where are we now?* (9–42). New York, NY: Peter Lang.

Rodriguez, N. S. (2018a). Hip-hop's authentic masculinity: A quare reading of Fox's *Empire. Television & New Media, 19*(3), 225–240.

Rodriguez, N. S. (2018b). Intersectionality & Latinx as digital disruptions of identity. TEDx Talks. https://www.youtube.com/watch?v=nUqqgMkC2T8.

Rodriguez, N. S., Huemmer, J., & Blumell, L. (2016). Mobile masculinities: An investigation of networked masculinities in gay dating apps. *Masculinities and Social Change, 5*(3), 241–267.

15

Exploring Intersectional Approaches to Pedagogy

Paromita Pain

Teaching a class on social media and its effects on society has been instrumental in showing me that students often can be naturally intersectional in their approach to learning. For example, discussions around online hatred of women invariably bring about questions that clearly demonstrate the relational richness of gender, sexuality, patriarchy, and oppression. In leading such discussions, I ensure that none of these concepts is encased in categories and addressed narrowly (Nash, 2008). As teachers and educators, how can we encourage such patterns of thinking and enhance the ability of students to naturally consider intersectional approaches?

Organizing pedagogy around an intersectional framework encourages nuanced explorations of how gender, race, and class interact, and helps students reframe concepts of society and politics. In the process, we can support incisive examinations of ubiquitous social and political structures. As we strengthen our understanding of differences, we will increase tolerance and develop an ability to stand up to and fight inequality. This chapter discusses and provides a road map to assist instructors in making approaches to intersectionality clear, identifying effective intersectional perspectives, and assisting learners to discern and delve into the different and inherent contradictions and tensions that shape different societal experiences. This chapter will identify and address common challenges of teaching and using intersectionality in classrooms.

INTERSECTIONALITY IN THE CLASSROOM

As a feminist, professor, and researcher, my work, revolving around alternative media's ability to empower the poor and powerless, scrutinizes how social class, culture, and gender influence notions of power. In my media-related classes, discussions centered around the inherent inequalities of the internet demand a consideration of technical and social hierarchies and power structures in the offline world that are often replicated in the online world.

For this chapter, I interviewed twenty professors teaching a variety of theoretical, research methods, and media-related classes to get practical perspectives on how such critical lenses and theories can be introduced. They discussed helping students understand the multiple and intersecting discriminations in the areas of race and gender and other concepts, as well as their different implications.

The interviewees teach undergraduate and graduate classes, ranging from purely journalism classes like reporting and writing and history of media to classes on gender, misogyny, race theory, and research methods. The latter classes often are cross-listed with various other liberal arts departments like history, anthropology, women's studies, and political science. In the interest of privacy, names and organizational information have been kept anonymous.

COMMON CHALLENGES

Most of the instructors agreed undergraduate students have little understanding of intersectionality. Students are generally exposed to such ideas at the college level and hence have little time to let the meanings sink. They often tended to look at experiences through a single lens. For example, as one professor with more than twenty years of experience said, "They understand (willingly and eagerly) that women were oppressed and exploited. But it takes a while for them to see how being Black and a woman has harder implications."

While graduate students certainly have more discernment toward such notions, it is often not "critical enough." One professor, teaching in a women and gender studies department at a midsize state university said, "They understand how gender and race might interact but often they don't see beyond the obvious." This was reiterated by a majority of respondents. Issues ranged from a lack of ability to see how intertwined social structures can be, to believing that social categories are watertight, and that discrimination is unidimensional in nature. A professor at a selective private university said:

Many students believe they know everything that there is to know about diversity, inclusion, and intersectionality, whether they use that term or not. While younger generations do tend to be more open, depending on where they come from and the location of the school they are attending, they often are not aware of their own unconscious biases. They also don't understand that people can become members of different communities, willingly or not. For example, a colleague can become a paraplegic after a skiing accident. He thus now is a member of the differently abled community in middle age, something he never expected. So he was now . . . an immigrant *and now* someone who many see as disabled.

Intersectionality as a theory is complex and it is important for instructors to delve in and clear nuances to themselves before entering the classroom. A professor who very consciously uses intersectionality in his classes said:

> We must first admit to ourselves that intersectionality is difficult. We often treat it as a sort of "fix." For example, we assume that understanding that gender and race are related is enough to resolve gender imbalances. This is a part of the problem. We must recognize that these are not issues that are fixed; rather, they are managed with the greater understanding that intersectionality brings.

THE RACE COLLISION

Teaching intersectionality as professors of color has its own set of challenges. It is clear that centering pedagogical design and practice through an intersectional lens supports the advancement of critical thinking that makes privilege and power structures obvious and visible (Case & Lewis, 2012). But what happens when the instructor's race is an obvious aspect of the connections that are being discussed? "Being Black and teaching intersectionality can often imply that your understanding and observations, especially about race and power relations, are personal and therefore unscientific," said one Black professor, who teaches in a midsize university with mostly white students. "It is very important to make clear that your lectures reflect social reality. Back up everything you say with facts. Use statistics. It's hard to argue numbers."

This also makes providing students feedback more effective. One professor at a private institution noted:

> When you are basing issues in research, students understand the value of detail. Students often assume that as long they are making connections, they are good to go. But they need to understand that the connections they make must be logical threads that will stand up to scrutiny. Intersectionality is not rhetorical fancy dance. Every conclusion must be backed up with fact.

Another issue not discussed much among instructors is how an emphasis on intersectional issues often negatively affects student evaluations. Issues of race and gender are often so basic as ideas that students often find it wearisome and challenging to think about them in-depth. One professor said this was a "fallout of making students think about issues that made them uncomfortable. Ideas that they have nurtured for most of their lives are suddenly being questioned."

ACKNOWLEDGING PERSONAL BIAS

A majority of my respondents said that a constructive way to begin would be to start by acknowledging "our own biases as people." One interviewee said:

> I always tend to look askance at women who change their names after they get married. I know I shouldn't. Everyone can make their own choice. That's part of what feminism gives us—the freedom to make our own choices. But I always ask, "why?" The answers are often disappointing. "It was really important to my husband," which is weak in my opinion, or "We want our whole family to have the same last name," which also doesn't make any sense. Again, I admit this is my personal weakness or bias, but at least I acknowledge it, which is step no. 1.

Instructors warn against "overloading" students with too many critical ideas at the start. A professor of media studies at a prominent state university said that a constructive approach here would involve making the nature of pedagogy intersectional and easing students in through class exercises. "For example, in a research methods class, students come in expecting to learn methods. Talking about research that explicitly shows how social issues of race and class can intersect and be valuable influences on the research questions is a useful way to ease in," she explained. She finds the resources in the "Toolkit for 'Teaching at the Intersections'" (2016) useful. "I especially like the films they have to make things from around the world familiar to my students," she says.

Another professor advised the use of examples that come up every day in the media. For example, the case of Tamir Rice (who was killed by police at age twelve) opens up discussions about race, power, and racism in the United States. "I sometimes draw on my own experiences as well, which is interesting given the age difference between me and my students," she said. Most recommended the use of examples that would immediately establish some sort of connection. The Tamir Rice case is at its heart about a child who was playing and who got shot. "When you introduce the example, emphasize that a child got shot, not randomly, not by accident, but by design because the police as an institution are extremely racist," she explained. "Students are shocked that children can be shot, and that's when you explain what it's like to be young, Black, and poor in the U.S. today."

CONSTRUCTIVE, NOT COMBATIVE

Conversations around intersectionality often make students defensive about their views. "I come from a very religious background myself, so I understand," said one respondent. She said being receptive about where the student came from is important in making conversations around the subject constructive and not combative. As instructors, she explained, we cannot emphasize our beliefs in the classroom nor show disagreement or disbelief no matter how outrageous the idea may seem. An approach that encourages the open sharing of thoughts generally leads to deeper understanding.

For younger students, especially those at the undergraduate level, defining what intersectionality is helps them parse the theory better. "Define concretely and with examples what social categories are, why they are necessary and how do they intersect with concrete examples, so that students can develop strong foundations to build on," said one professor from a large state university. He uses the *Oxford English Dictionary* meaning and carries a dictionary with him to physically show students and encourages them to keep this definition in mind as they start thinking about their concerns. "It provides for a concrete start," he said.

SAFE SPACES

Creating safe spaces where students can express emotions and ask questions is often key. One professor in a midsize state university said that she taught intersectionality by using different aspects of embodied practices like theater. She realized early on that students come in with a repertoire of defenses about how they will engage with the subject. "I make them hold hands and look into each other's eyes. Suddenly they are faced with something that does not have to be reacted to but rather something that requires a response in a very immediate way. For when we hold hands, we immediately notice things like body temperature, moisture, and texture of skin," she said.

This can be emotional, either positive or negative, and while students don't always express their feelings, it happens. There is often nervous laughter and she helps them recognize that this laughter is their reflex reaction to unmediated experiences like holding a stranger's hand. "I explain how their emotional, physical, and reflex reactions are all interrelated, and this gets us out of the hyperintellectual approach that we often take toward ideas of intersectionality," she said. Holding hands and connecting with another student creates associations that help make students feel safe to ask questions and share different experiences.

Intersectionality is about inclusion and diversity, but often classrooms do not reflect national diversity. Thus, explaining how disadvantages overlap and are compounded can be tricky. A way to approach this, explained one interviewee, would be to use a simple example of what we omit when we focus on one thing. For example, the interviewee said:

> As I look at you, I don't look at the door. Why do I make the choices that I do? [In this] case I cannot look at the door because I am looking at you. What dictates choices? How do choices work in social settings?

It is important to emphasize that intersectionality is an important part of the human experience. "Begin by talking about human relationships to stuff like food, clothes, culture, and emphasize, right at the outset, that what is important are human relations and that human relations are imperfect and messy," said one professor from a large state university. As Kimberlé Crenshaw has long asserted, "Intersectionality was a lived reality before it became a term" (Crenshaw, 2015, p. 215).

Examining intersectionality through a map of shared experiences also helps. For example, one professor from a large state university said that in a class on criminology he has students create maps of crimes in the United States and compare them with crimes in other countries. Class discussion centers around whether other countries share the same characteristics and why some attributes are similar but not others.

Using history to create a rich context around issues is an integral part of most teaching plans. This context can also be used to answer the challenges raised by students. One professor at a large state university said that while her students would not directly question her in class, sometimes white males would push back against the idea of gender discrimination. "They would often say . . . why haven't women sorted out issues of pay gaps yet and why do they work for such low wages," she said. "We would then start to historically trace the evolution of discrimination and work to understand how gender discrimination is many faceted." It is also important here to understand the complete story. For example, while women in general get lower pay than men, women of color are paid lower than white women.

One professor said that her classes dealing with religious identities online are always naturally intersectional. So she makes "really concerted efforts" to get to know her students. "Once I know about their back-grounds, I am very respectful about the issues I bring up in class. I make sure my terminology is right and each concept is explained thoroughly before we move on."

Clear-cut examples help students anchor their thought process and introduce the concepts as organic growths from class discussions. This reduces ambiguity about the idea and the student's stance on it. Depend-ing on the level of student understanding, issues of intersectionality can be given further thought as part of class and homework assignments. Getting to know students also means getting to know about their identi-ties. "I did not know I had a transgender student in class," she said. "The minute I came to know, I immediately ensured that we were using pre-ferred pronouns, addressing the student the way they wanted to and with sensitivity toward their needs." This sends out a message to the rest of the students that diversity matters and will be respected.

Respect, beginning with valuing student views, was a point many respondents underlined. Teaching intersectionality begins with the creation of a classroom that welcomes different views. "The university makes us include the generic lines about how we must be respectful of each other in [our] syllabus," said one professor at a small liberal arts college. "But I always make clear in my class, on the first day, that all opinions are welcome. I don't talk about the respect aspect but imply it through all class conversations and interactions that we have. That makes students feel that they can share their thoughts and are more willing to rethink their ideas."

As professors often observe, students mostly try to find answers to general questions, such as how to make America more diverse or bridge gender inequalities. The focus, as one respondent said, "Was all about finding the right answer!" Students want to use intersectionality to get to the answer quickly and often use notions of intersectionality to draw false conclusions. For example, a common misstep is to group all marginalized groups together, and so students assume, if this is the Black experience, then we can say that it is the same for the Native American experience. They refuse to critically look at how the physical body is categorized across different groups. As educators, we must beware of gross over-generalizations. Intersectionality is about similarities, but it is also about the multitudes of other scenarios. Intersectionality does not override the uniqueness of individual experience.

Echoing this line of thought, another participant said that she also uses intersectionality to show students that connections between two seem-ingly unrelated ideas like heart surgery and engineering may exist but that does not mean that all connections are valid. "Research principles of reliability and validity must be rigorously applied here," she said.

This is also a chance to encourage students to think about issues that will always be outside their realm of experience and the ways things are usually categorized. "We must encourage students here to break out [of] the narrow constraints in which we put even education in," said one participant. "We expect students to go to school and learn a narrow set of skills to apply in a specific field. Through an intersectional lens we can help students critically evaluate even the education they are getting and that is always a great starting point." For example, this interviewee starts his class on technical writing by talking about what defines good writing and the applications of being able to conceptualize and write well across all fields. Students are encouraged to explore different genres of writing and see how certain styles work, even if it's for a few early classes, before they turn their attention to purely technical writing.

Explaining the many different facets of the theory can be difficult since each student will approach it uniquely and thus have different questions. Discussions at times will have to be individual in nature to resolve doubts and encourage critical thinking. In large lecture courses this can be a problem. *Teaching Media Quarterly* offers specific lessons plans for large classes with various questions that can be explored to pique interest and introduce the subject (see https://pubs.lib.umn.edu/index.php/tmq/article/view/1054).

Another aspect that is often ignored is that change in social structures and the ways we think are inevitable and thus intersections among social categories too will undergo transformations. Coined by legal scholar Kimberlé Crenshaw in 1989, intersectionality as a term has also been criticized for leading to much "backlash and confusion" (Emba, 2015). Thus, "we must understand that social intersections are not set in stone and must be negotiated and renegotiated as time goes on," as one professor at a teaching university explained. The role of educational institutions is important. Some believe that students from elementary school onward must be and need to be made aware of intersectional issues. Also, universities must play a greater role in fostering classes that are naturally intersectional in nature. "We often tend to think that as a theory it is applicable to only gender and race related classes," explained one professor from a large public university. "But that creates a fence about it. Intersectionality can be used in every field and intersectional approaches must be made a matter of norm if we are to really work toward a more equitable society."

TIPS AND TRICKS TO TEACH INTERSECTIONALITY

The instructors I interviewed shared some of their tips for using and encouraging more intersectional thought in the classroom.

1. A variation on a Poynter Institute exercise called "Peeling the Onion" involves making a list of how people may identify themselves. For example, a young college student might list college student, sorority member, newspaper staff member, journalism major, daughter, sister, and so on. It depends on how they identify. But this identity is different for every person and can change over time. Later, someone may say their identity is mother, spouse, daughter, sister, Latina, friend, educator, journalist, diversity advocate, and so forth. Clearly, it has changed from me first to family first.

2. Pop-up newsrooms. This is a method some universities use in introductory journalism classes. Students go out in groups of three and set up a table and chairs in specific neighborhoods to try and learn what the important issues are to members of that community. They are encouraged to set up in parks, church parking lots, mall parking lots, and other locations. This is intersectionality in action.

3. Classroom resources from *Teaching Tolerance* provide various teaching guides and lesson plans, available at https://www.tolerance.org/classroom-resources/teaching-strategies.

4. The low-hanging fruit is the journalism "diet" students are required to consume during the semester. Professors often post articles to discuss that are tied to the class subject, but also happen to focus on diversity and intersectionality to keep it in the conversation.

5. Some professors explain how everything has to do with human experience. For example, in an engineering class, as some professors talk about technology, they discuss how some people will experience ordinary things, such as ordering food online, differently because they have access to technology, while others will not know anything about it because they lack it. How is access defined? And is access a singular concept or is it defined by political, economic, and technical issues?

6. Some professors in their intro classes use BuzzFeed's "How Privileged Are You" quiz to introduce the idea. It's BuzzFeed; students are usually aware of it and comfortable with taking quizzes on it. Suddenly, issues of race and sexuality seem more accessible. It helps them lower their guard and it can lead to important discussions.

One professor has a module on the Maynard Institute's Fault Lines approach to introducing diversity in her diversity courses and she finds that it is a good way to introduce the concept of intersectionality. She also uses it in other classes she teaches. Dori J. Maynard, president of the Maynard Institute for Journalism Education in Oakland, California, based her five fault lines of race, class, gender, generation, and geography on her father Robert C. Maynard's philosophy because he believed they were the most enduring forces that have shaped social tensions since the founding of this nation. The Fault Lines approach can be downloaded from http://media -diversity.org/en/additional-files/documents/Z%20Current%20 MDI%20Resources/How%20inclusive%20is%20your%20cover age%20%5BEN%5D.pdf.

7. For their undergraduate classes, some instructors use lesson plans from PBS Learning Media, which has various lesson plans that help students examine the concept of intersectionality as it applies to building inclusive social groups and movements and different other situations. This can be found at https://ca.pbslearningmedia .org/subjects/english-language-arts-and-literacy/informational -texts/integration-of-knowledge-and-ideas/diverse-formats-and -media/#.XhJsIkdKhPY.

8. The Institute for Humane Education (https://humaneeducation .org/blog/2017/resources-teaching-learning-intersectionality/) has various useful resources.

9. The *Washington Post*'s, "Intersectionality" (https://www.washing tonpost.com/news/in-theory/wp/2015/09/21/intersectionality -a-primer/?utm_term=.c1e8285c4fb3) is a must-use in my journalism class. It is done by a well-known mainstream newspaper and it helps students understand the importance of intersectional work in journalism.

REFERENCES

Bowleg, L. (2012). The problem with the phrase women and minorities: Intersectionality—an important theoretical framework for public health. *American Journal of Public Health, 102*(7), 1267–1273.

Case, K. A., & Lewis, M. K. (2012). Teaching intersectional LGBT psychology: Reflections from historically Black and Hispanic-serving universities. *Psychology & Sexuality, 3*(3), 260–276.

Crenshaw, K. (2015, September 24). Why intersectionality can't wait. Retrieved June 20, 2019, from https://www.washingtonpost.com/news/in-theory/ wp/2015/09/24/why-intersectionality-cant-wait/?utm_term=.b2215a47b552.

Emba, C. (2015, September 21). Intersectionality. *The Washington Post.* Retrieved June 20, 2019, from https://www.washingtonpost.com/news/in-theory/ wp/2015/09/21/intersectionality-a-primer/?utm_term=.3a64c6b23e5f.

Nash, J. C. (2008). Re-thinking intersectionality. *Feminist Review, 89*(1), 1–15. Retrieved from https://journals.sagepub.com/doi/10.1057/fr.2008.4.

Toolkit for "Teaching at the Intersections." (2016). *Teaching Tolerance, 53*(Summer). Retrieved from https://www.tolerance.org/magazine/summer-2016/toolkit -for-teaching-at-the-intersections.

16

🌀

Recommendations

Diversify the Classroom, Diversify the Newsroom

Candi Carter Olson and Tracy Everbach

As we are writing this conclusion, the U.S. House has started an impeachment investigation against President Donald Trump. The #MeToo movement is marking its two-year anniversary, a feat of movement survival almost unparalleled in contemporary digital society. A shooting that killed two in Germany was watched live by almost 2,200 viewers on Twitch. Turkey is invading Syria after U.S. defense forces withdrew from the region, leaving our former allies, the Kurds, undefended.

The news cycle keeps turning. As it turns, journalism and mass communication professionals and academics alike will increasingly be called upon to cover challenging topics with depth, context, and insight.

As college campuses and American society become increasingly diverse, it is incumbent upon media sources to provide varied and comprehensive coverage of traditionally disenfranchised communities. One of the first steps that needs to happen is for newsrooms themselves to become more diverse. This is not a new problem. The 1968 Kerner Commission report found that "our nation is moving toward two societies, one black, one white—separate and unequal" (Kerner Commission, 1968, p. 1). Today, this statement could be updated to say that our nation is moving toward a multitude of divisions based upon identity fault lines, those of race, class, gender, sexuality, and ability perhaps being the most obvious currently. However, also today, "at least eight out of 10 Americans view diversity as 'at least somewhat important' in the workplace. Yet 50 years after Kerner, we still see chronic underrepresentation of racial and ethnic minorities in print and broadcast media" (Cobb, 2018, para. 6). This underrepresentation extends to internet media. Across all media sources, whites represented 77 percent of the workforce, according to a Pew Research Center analysis of 2012–2016 American Community Survey data. This is more than 10 percent higher than the general working population, where whites still dominate at about 65 percent of the overall workforce (Grieco, 2018, para. 2).

Why does diversity in the newsroom matter, though, if stories still are being told? Writer and humanitarian Chimamanda Ngozi Adichie told attendees at the Conrad N. Hilton Humanitarian Symposium and Prize Ceremony that a single viewpoint does not tell the whole story about a group of people. She recounted a professor who had once told her that she did not tell "authentic" Nigerian stories because her stories focused on the middle class, not the poorest Nigerians. She said, "This is how to create a single story. Show people as just one thing, over and over again, until they become that thing." By bringing diverse voices to the forefront and allowing people to tell their individual authentic stories, the picture of humanity becomes richer and more humane: "To give people the opportunity to tell their stories in their own language is to give them their dignity," she said (Rios, 2019, para. 1–4).

Perhaps more to the point, the American Press Institute asserts, "Journalism, in its truest form, should be produced for the benefit of all, not only those who wield a particular power, class or authority" (Kovac-Ashley, 2019, para. 9).

This is another place where the Kerner Commission's work was prescient. The Kerner Commission recognized in 1968 the importance of diversifying newsrooms to produce accurate coverage of minority issues. The authors urged the news media to "cooperate in the establishment of a privately organized and funded Institute of Urban Communications to train and educate journalists in urban affairs, recruit and train more Negro journalists, develop methods for improving police-press relations, review coverage of riots and racial issues, and support continuing research in the urban field" (Kerner Commission, 1968, p. 18). The authors saw that bringing journalists into newsrooms and training them would produce more thoughtful, accurate, and distinct news reports on a range of stories of interest to disenfranchised groups.

Journalism classrooms are the obvious spaces for providing media literacy training to sundry students, giving them the tools and empowering them to tell stories about counterculture and alienated publics. University-age students are in prime identity-development years. This is a time when they will differentiate themselves from their parents, and they will also learn to affiliate with groups that comprise their identities, such as racial and ethnic groups, different disability groups, and gender and sexual identity groups. These group affiliations give students rulers for self-evaluation. "Students often reported evaluating themselves in relation to their co-ethnic peer group. When this self-evaluation was positive, it encouraged students to learn more about group history or language. When it was negative, students expressed feelings of ethnic inadequacy" (Ortiz & Santos, 2010, para. 11).

Students will encounter stories about their identity groups in journalism and mass communication classrooms through reading the news and affiliating with the increasingly diverse student body that comprises today's college campuses. Avoiding the issues harms not only the students, but also the learning environment they require to become empowered, thoughtful journalists. The journalists of the future will tell stories about diverse groups, particularly as digital media provides a proliferation of new outlets for people who are not part of the mainstream media. The challenge will come in amplifying those voices outside of niche market publications. That's where journalism training programs come in. Just as the Kerner Commission saw the value in training Black people to tell stories about Black people's lived experiences, so journalism programs need to see the value in showing students how to ethically tell the stories of diverse people in mainstream news outlets.

Diversity and the push to tell diverse stories responsibly is becoming a focal point of many journalism programs across the United States. The University of Arizona's School of Journalism includes this statement on their public Diversity and Inclusion site: "The School of Journalism faculty members and staff believe diversity and inclusion are essential to bettering journalism and society. . . . Diverse views are critical in journalism" (School of Journalism, 2017, para. 1). This focus on diversity has never had a better ecosystem for taking root among our journalism and mass communication schools. While President Trump's tenure has brought increased criticism of the media and created an environment in which journalists have been physically and verbally attacked, it also has driven increasing interest in media programs across the United States, a surge that some journalism faculty and administrators have termed the "Trump bump" (Pettway, 2019, para. 6).

The irony of a Trump bump is not lost on any of us, but the opportunity may be lost if we don't see it and capture it. Students are eager to engage in tough topics. They want to have open conversations that challenge their worldviews. We hope this book has given you new tools and perspectives for engaging in those conversations in new and insightful ways. Following this chapter is a list of resources—books, films, articles, websites—that you can use to engage students and start conversations. May both our students and we see tough topics as opportunities and not roadblocks to greater understanding of how media operates to show us a sometimes skewed and monochromatic view of ourselves and others.

REFERENCES

Cobb, J. (2018, November 5). When newsrooms are dominated by white people, they miss crucial facts. *The Guardian* Retrieved from https://www.theguardian.com/world/commentisfree/2018/nov/05/newsroom-diversity-media-race-journalism.

Grieco, E. (2018). Newsroom employees are less diverse than U.S. workers overall. Pew Research Center. Retrieved from https://www.pewresearch.org/fact-tank/2018/11/02/newsroom-employees-are-less-diverse-than-u-s-workers-overall/.

Kerner Commission. (1968). Report of the national advisory commission on civil disorders. Retrieved from http://www.eisenhowerfoundation.org/docs/kerner.pdf.

Kovac-Ashley, A. (2019). Diversity and inclusivity in journalism. *American Press Institute*. Retrieved from https://www.americanpressinstitute.org/diversity-programs/.

Ortiz, A. M., & Santos, S. J. (2010). Campus diversity and ethnic identity development. *Diversity and Democracy*. Association of American Colleges and Universities. Retrieved from https://www.aacu.org/publications-research/periodicals/campus-diversity-and-ethnic-identity-development.

Pettway, A. (2019). Previously on the decline, journalism school enrollment benefits from 'Trump Bump.' *Insight into Diversity*. Retrieved from https://www.insightintodiversity.com/previously-on-the-decline-journalism-school-enrollment-benefits-from-trump-bump/.

Rios, C. (2019). The danger of the single story—at our borders and in our movements. *Ms.* Retrieved from https://msmagazine.com/2019/10/21/the-danger-of-a-single-story-at-our-borders-and-in-our-movements/?fbclid=IwAR1WRAoRtnOgHQ-OPsOKCo0ClpEvVgDBj-GfVWar-Bg7RaAPTiVXu_iqFtE.

School of Journalism. (2017). Diversity and inclusion. Retrieved from https://journalism.arizona.edu/diversity.

List of Classroom Resources

Building an Integrated/ Intersectional Journalism Classroom

SUGGESTED TEXTBOOKS

Bramblett-Solomon, S., & Carstarphen, M. (2017). *Race, gender, class and media: Studying mass communication and multiculturalism*. Dubuque, IA: Kendall Hunt.

Davis, A. Y. (2011). *Women, race & class*. New York, NY: Vintage.

Dines, G., Humez, J. M., Yousman, W. E., & Bindig, L. B. (2017). *Gender, race, and class in media* (5th ed.). New York, NY: Sage.

Lind, R. A. (2019). *Race/gender/class/media: Considering diversity across audiences, content, and producers* (4th ed.). New York, NY: Routledge.

SUPPLEMENTARY BOOKS

Armstrong, C. (2014). *Media disparity: A gender battleground*. Lanham, MD: Lexington Books.

Benshoff, H., & Griffin. S. (2009). *America on film: Representing race, class, gender, and sexuality at the movies* (2nd ed.). Hoboken, NJ: Wiley-Blackwell.

Coates, T. (2015). *Between the world and me*. New York, NY: Spiegel & Grau.

Creedon, P., & Cramer, J. (2007). *Women in mass communication* (3rd ed.). Los Angeles, CA: Sage.

D'Angelo, R. (2018). *White fragility: Why it's so hard for white people to talk about racism*. Boston, MA: Beacon Press.

Dines, G., & Humez, J. M. (2014). *Gender, race, and class in media: A critical reader* (4th ed.). Los Angeles, CA: Sage.

Entman, R. M., & Rojecki, A. (2001). *The black image in the white mind: Media and race in America*. Chicago, IL: University of Chicago Press.

Freire, P. (1970). *Pedagogy of the oppressed* (Ramos, MB, Trans.). New York, NY: Continuum.

Gilger, K. G., & Wallace, J. (2019). *There's no crying in newsrooms: What women have learned about what it takes to lead.* Lanham, MD: Rowman & Littlefield.

Gross, L., & Woods, J. (1999). *The Columbia reader on lesbians and gay men in media, society, and politics.* New York, NY: Columbia University Press.

Hains, R. C. (2012). *The princess problem: Guiding our girls through the princess-obsessed years.* Chicago: Sourcebooks.

Hooks, b. (2008). *Reel to real: Race, sex, and class at the movies.* New York, NY: Routledge.

Messner, M. A. (2002). *Taking the field: Women, men and sports.* Minneapolis: University of Minnesota Press.

Orenstein, P. (2012). *Cinderella ate my daughter: Dispatches from the front lines of the new girlie-girl culture.* New York, NY: Harper Collins.

Orenstein, P. (2013). *Schoolgirls: Young women, self-esteem, and the confidence gap.* New York, NY: Anchor.

Rakow, L. F., & Wackwitz, L. A. (2004). *Feminist communication theory: Selections in context.* Thousand Oaks, CA: Sage.

Reichert, T., & Lambiase J. (2006). *Sex in consumer culture: The erotic content of media and marketing.* New York, NY: Erlbaum.

Vickery, J. R., & Everbach, T. (2018). *Mediating misogyny: Gender, technology and harassment.* Cham, Switzerland: Palgrave MacMillan.

Wilson, C., Gutierrez, F., & Chao, L. (2013). *Racism, sexism, and the media: Multicultural issues into the new communication age* (4th ed.). Los Angeles, CA: Sage.

DOCUMENTARIES AND FEATURE FILMS

13th. (2016). Kandoo Films, Forward Movement.

Get Out. (2017). Universal Pictures.

Killing Us Softly 4: Advertising's Image of Women. (2010). Media Education Foundation.

Latinos Beyond Reel: Challenging a Media Stereotype. (2013). Media Education Foundation.

Mickey Mouse Monopoly: Disney, Childhood and Corporate Power. (2001). Media Education Foundation. (Update may be coming.)

Miss Representation. (2011). The Representation Project.

Moonlight. (2016). A24.

Not Just a Game: Power, Politics and American Sports. (2010). Media Education Foundation.

Pariah. (2011). Focus Features.

Paris Is Burning. (1990). Off-White productions.

Rent. (2005). Sony Pictures.

The Birdcage. (1996). Nichols Film Company.

The Black Press: Soldiers Without Swords. (1999). The Chicago Production Center at WTTW.

The Celluloid Closet. (1995). Sony Pictures Classics.

The Mask You Live In. (2015). The Representation Project.

To Wong Foo, Thanks for Everything! Julie Newmar. (1995). Amblin Entertainment.
Tough Guise 2: Violence, Manhood & American Culture. (2013). Media Education Foundation.
White Like Me: Race, Racism and White Privilege in America. (2013). Media Education Foundation.
Y Tu Mamá También. (2001). 20th Century Fox.

TED TALKS AND OTHER ONLINE VIDEOS

ABC News. (2013, July 21). *Anti-Muslim harassment: What would you do? Islamophobia.* [Video file.] Retrieved from https://www.youtube.com/watch?v=Lk7GYyAWOaY.
Adichie, C. N. (2017, April 14). *Chimamanda Ngozi Adichie: We should all be feminists.* [Video file]. Retrieved from https://www.ted.com/talks/chimamanda_ngozi_adichie_we_should_all_be_feminists?language=en.
Josh Leyva's YouTube channel, featuring Gaylo videos: https://www.youtube.com/channel/UClO7jPUJTldmuf3hl1BMtUQ.
Key, K. M., & Peele, J. (2013, October 9). *Hoodie.* [Video file.] Retrieved from https://www.youtube.com/watch?v=ztRSm_SJP58.
PBS. (2013). *Media coverage & female athletes.* [Video file.] Retrieved from https://video.tpt.org/video/tpt-co-productions-media-coverage-female-athletes/.
Porter, T. (2010). *A call to men.* [Video file.] Retrieved from https://www.ted.com/talks/tony_porter_a_call_to_men.
Russell, C. (2013, February 4). *Cameron Russell: Looks aren't everything. Believe me, I'm a model.* [Video file.] Retrieved from https://www.ted.com/talks/cameron_russell_looks_aren_t_everything_believe_me_i_m_a_model.
Steiner, L. M. (2013, January 25). *Leslie Morgan Steiner: Why domestic violence victims don't leave.* [Video file.] Retrieved from https://www.ted.com/talks/leslie_morgan_steiner_why_domestic_violence_victims_don_t_leave?language=en.
World of Wonder's WOWPresents YouTube channel: https://www.youtube.com/user/WOWPresents.
Young, S. (2014). *I'm not your inspiration, thank you very much.* [Video file.] Retrieved from https://www.ted.com/talks/stella_young_i_m_not_your_inspiration_thank_you_very_much?language=en.
Zayid, M. (2014). *I got 99 problems . . . palsy is just one.* [Video file.] Retrieved from https://www.youtube.com/watch?v=buRLc2eWGPQ.

ARTICLES

Andrews, S. (2008, September 29). Who is Wall Street's Queen B? *Vanity Fair.* http://www.vanityfair.com/politics/features/2008/11/moneyhoney200811.
Emba, C. (2015). Intersectionality. *The Washington Post.* Retrieved from https://www.washingtonpost.com/news/in-theory/wp/2015/09/21/intersectionality-a-primer/.
Hentrick, N. (2018). Always already intersectional: Introducing intersectionality in large lecture courses. *Teaching Media Quarterly* 6(2). Retrieved from https://pubs.lib.umn.edu/index.php/tmq/article/view/1054.

List of Classroom Resources

Jha, R., & Wesely, T. (2014). How privileged are you? Buzzfeed. Retrieved from buzzfeed.com/regajha/how-privileged-are-you.

Maynard Institute for Journalism Education. (n.d.). Reality checks content analysis kit. Retrieved from http://media-diversity.org/en/additional-files/documents/Z%20Current%20MDI%20Resources/How%20inclusive%20is%20your%20coverage%20%5BEN%5D.pdf.

National Institute for Health. (2011). Your guide to healthy sleep. https://www.nhlbi.nih.gov/files/docs/public/sleep/healthy_sleep.pdf.

New York Times Magazine. (2019, August 18). The 1619 project. https://www.nytimes.com/interactive/2019/08/14/magazine/1619-america-slavery.html.

Owens, L. C. (2008). Network news: The role of race in source selection and story topic. *Howard Journal of Communications, 19*(4), 355–370. DOI: 10.1080/10646170802418269.

Pulitzer Center. (2019). The 1619 project: Curricular materials. http://www.pulitzercenter.org/lesson-plan-grouping/1619-project-curriculum.

Reisman, A., & Dahl, M. (2015). This is your brain on advertising: Why sex doesn't sell. *New York Magazine.* Retrieved from http://nymag.com/scienceofus/2015/10/why-sex-doesnt-sell.html.

Women's Media Center. (2015). Writing rape: How the U.S. media cover campus rape and sexual assault. http://www.womensmediacenter.com/reports/writing-rape-how-u-s-media-cover-campus-rape-and-sexual-assault.

PODCASTS

On the Media: https://www.wnycstudios.org/podcasts/otm.

NPR's *Code Switch:* https://www.npr.org/podcasts/510312/codeswitch.

Latino's Who Lunch: http://www.latinoswholunch.com/.

Latino USA: https://www.latinousa.org/full-shows/.

PRI's *Otherhood:* https://www.pri.org/programs/otherhood.

Disability After Dark: http://www.andrewgurza.com/podcast.

Black, Trans, and Beautiful: https://podcasts.apple.com/us/podcast/black-trans-beautiful/id1361445893.

Bitter Brown Femmes: https://bitterbrownfemmespodcast.com/.

WEBSITES AND INTERNET RESOURCES

American Association of University Professors: https://www.aaup.org/.

Center for Public Integrity: https://publicintegrity.org/.

College Media Association: http://www.collegemedia.org/

Dart Center for Journalism & Trauma: https://dartcenter.org/.

Domestic Violence Awareness Project. (2018). Engaging the media. National Resource Center on Domestic Violence: https://nrcdv.org/dvam/engaging-the-media.

Geena Davis Institute on Gender in Media: https://seejane.org/.

GLAAD Media Institute: https://www.glaad.org/institute.

Institute for Humane Education: https://humaneeducation.org/blog/2017/ resources-teaching-learning-intersectionality/.

Jim Crow Museum of Racist Memorabilia at Ferris State University: https://www .ferris.edu/jimcrow/.

Native American Journalists Association AP Style Guide Insert: https://najanews room.com/ap-style-insert/.

Native American Journalists Association Bingo Card: https://najanewsroom.com/ bingo-card/.

Native American Journalists Association Indigenous Investigative Collective: https://najanewsroom.com/2019/02/11/naja-launches-indigenous-inves tigative-collective/.

Native American Journalists Association Red Press Initiative: https://najanews room.com/2019/04/09/naja-launches-survey-to-assess-press-freedom-in -indian-country/.

Native American Journalists Association Reporting Guides: https://najanews room.com/reporting-guides/.

Native American Journalists Association Student Chapters: https://najanews room.com/college-chapters/.

PBS Learning Media Diverse Formats and Media informational texts: https:// www.pbslearningmedia.org/subjects/english-language-arts-and-literacy/ informational-texts/integration-of-knowledge-and-ideas/diverse-formats -and-media/.

RAINN: https://www.rainn.org.

Student Press Law Center: https://splc.org/.

PROFESSIONAL ORGANIZATIONS

Association for Education in Journalism and Mass Communication (AEJMC) Commission on the Status of Women: https://aejmc.us/csw/.

AEJMC Commission on the Status of Minorities: https://csmdiversity.org/.

American Advertising Federation: https://www.aaf.org/.

American Association of University Women: https://www.aauw.org/.

Asian American Journalists Association: https://www.aaja.org/.

Association for Women in Communications: https://www.womcom.org/.

Consortium of Higher Education LGBT Resource Professionals: https://www .lgbtcampus.org/.

Disabled Writers: https://disabledwriters.com.

Hispanic Association of Colleges and Universities: https://www.hacu.net/hacu/ default.asp.

Journalism and Women Symposium: https://www.jaws.org/.

National Association of Black Journalists: https://www.nabj.org/.

National Association of Hispanic Journalists: https://nahj.org/.

National Center on Disability and Journalism: https://ncdj.org/.

National Press Photographers Association: https://nppa.org/.

Native American Journalists Association: https://najanewsroom.com/.

Public Relations Society of America: https://www.prsa.org/

Society for Professional Journalists: https://www.spj.org/

Index

179

About the Editors
and Contributors

EDITORS

Candi Carter Olson is an associate professor at Utah State University. Her research interests focus on women's press clubs as agents of change, newswomen's history, and women's use of social media to build community and organize activist groups. She is a 2018 AEJMC Rising Scholar Research Award winner, and in the past received an American Association of University Women American Fellowship, a Mountain West Center research grant, and an *American Journalism* Rising Scholar award. *Underserved Communities and Digital Discourse: Getting Voices Heard,* a book she coedited with Victoria L. LaPoe and Benjamin LaPoe, was published in October 2018. She has published in *Journalism & Mass Communication Quarterly,* the *Journal of Communication Inquiry, Journalism History, American Journalism, Feminist Media Studies, Pennsylvania History,* and *Media Report to Women.* Additionally, she has a coauthored a book chapter in the 2018 *Mediating Misogyny: Gender, Technology, and Harassment.* Carter Olson received her PhD in communication from the University of Pittsburgh. She is a past head of the Association for Education in Journalism and Mass Communication (AEJMC) Commission on the Status of Women.

Tracy Everbach is a professor of journalism in the Mayborn School of Journalism at the University of North Texas. She teaches undergraduate and graduate classes on race, gender, and media; news reporting; mass communication theories; and qualitative research methods. Her research focuses on women's work and leadership in journalism, and on representations of race and gender in media. She is the coeditor of *Mediating Misogyny: Gender Technology and Harassment* (2018). Her work also has been published in *Journalism & Mass Communication Quarterly, Newspaper Research Journal, Journal of Sports Media, Journal of Communication Inquiry, Electronic News, Media Report to Women, Columbia Journalism Review,* and *American Journalism.* She is the 2019 winner of the Donna Allen Award for Feminist Advocacy from AEJMC. She received her PhD in journalism from the University of Missouri-Columbia. She is a former newspaper reporter, including twelve years on the city news desk at *The Dallas Morning News.* She is a past head of the Association for Education in Journalism and Mass Communication (AEJMC) Commission on the Status of Women. She currently is a member of the AEJMC Standing Committee on Teaching.

CONTRIBUTORS

Laura Castañeda is a professor of professional practice at the University of Southern California's Annenberg School for Communication and Journalism. Her research interests focus on Latinx issues, gender issues, and journalism education. Her freelance work about Latina issues and invisible disabilities has been published in *USA Today's Hispanic Living* magazine, TheAtlantic.com, MediaShift, and *Columbia Journalism Review,* among others. Scholarly papers have appeared in *Journalism & Mass Communication Educator* and *Journalism Studies.* Castañeda is the coeditor of *News and Sexuality: Media Portraits of Diversity* (2005). She is the coauthor of *The Latino Guide to Personal Money Management,* published in 1999 and released in Spanish in 2001. She earned undergraduate degrees in journalism and international affairs from the University of Southern California, a master's degree from Columbia University's School of International and Public Affairs, and a doctorate from the USC Rossier School of Education. She also was awarded a Knight-Bagehot Fellowship in business and economics reporting from Columbia's School of Journalism. Castañeda was awarded the Association for Education in Journalism and Mass Communication's 2002 Baskett Mosse Award for Faculty Development. Before teaching, Castañeda worked as a reporter, editor, and columnist at the Associated Press, *The Dallas Morning News,* and *The San Francisco Chronicle.*

Meredith D. Clark is an assistant professor in the Department of Media Studies at the University of Virginia. Her research focuses on the intersections of race, media, and power with an emphasis on news media processes and social media audiences. In 2015, she was named one of the 100 Most Influential African Americans under 40 for her research on Black Twitter. She was one of the founding contributors of Poynter.org's diversity column and spent ten years in the news industry as a reporter, columnist, and editor before pursuing an academic career. She formerly served as head of the AEJMC Commission on the Status of Women.

Khadija Ejaz recently graduated with a doctoral degree in mass communication from the University of South Carolina and worked as an assistant professor at Barry University, Miami Shores, Florida. Her research interests include critical theory, with much of her work centered on the study of gender and postcolonialism. Her dissertation is a critical analysis of news coverage of the controversies around brain death in the Jahi McMath case as it was covered in newspapers in California. Khadija has been published in the *Journal of Communication Inquiry, Journal of Gender Studies,* and *Journalism Practice* and has served as the instructor of record for undergraduate courses in research methods and writing. She is also active in the Association for Education in Journalism and Mass Communications, Broadcast Education Association, and International Communication Association. Her previous career was in information technology. She has also written several children's books that were published in the United States, one of which won the South Asia Book Award in 2016.

Steve Fox is a senior lecturer and director of the Sports Journalism Concentration in the Journalism Department at the University of Massachusetts Amherst. He founded the concentration and is also faculty advisor for the annual Women in Sports Media Symposium—a one-day gathering of women students and women professionals in the field of sports media. Steve has been a professional journalist for more than thirty years as both an editor and reporter, covering sports, politics, and other news. Prior to joining the UMass journalism department in 2007 he worked at various publications, including *The Washington Post* website for ten years where he worked on both the sports and national desks. He continues to write columns for both local and national publications and lectures extensively on news literacy and news ethics.

Rebecca C. Hains is a professor of media and communication at Salem State University in Massachusetts. She has authored two books—*Growing Up With Girl Power: Girlhood on Screen and in Everyday Life* (2012) and *The Princess Problem: Guiding Our Girls Through the Princess-Obsessed Years* (2014)—and coedited the anthologies *Princess Cultures: Mediating Girls' Identities and Imaginations* (2015) and *Cultural Studies of LEGO: More Than Just Bricks* (2019). Her previous research on children's media culture has appeared in scholarly anthologies including *Geek Chic: Smart Women in*

Popular Culture (ed. Inness, 2007), *Women in Popular Culture: Representation and Meaning* (2008) and *Mediated Girlhoods: New Explorations of Girls' Media Culture* (2011). Her work has appeared in scholarly journal articles including *Women's Studies in Communication* and *Popular Communication.* Hains has presented peer-reviewed papers on children's media culture at the major conferences in her field, including those of the International Communication Association (ICA), the National Communication Association (NCA), and the National Women's Studies Association (NWSA). She is a past board member of both ICA and NWSA and spearheaded the formation of the Girls Studies Interest Group at NWSA. She has been interviewed as an expert commentator in a range of media, including NPR's *On Point*, BBC News, *The Meredith Vieira Show*, and documentary films. She has also served as a guest contributor, writing on media culture for publications such as *The Christian Science Monitor*, *The Washington Post*, and *The Boston Globe Magazine.*

Meg Heckman is an assistant professor of journalism at Northeastern University in Boston where she teaches a mix of graduate and undergraduate classes that support students in cultivating digitally relevant skills in verification, story craft, and audience engagement. She is also the advisor for *The Scope*, a student-run experimental digital magazine devoted to telling stories of justice, hope, and resilience. She spent more than a decade as a reporter and, later, the digital editor at the *Concord (NH) Monitor* and continues to work as an occasional consultant for local news organizations. She writes regularly for a variety of publications about the intersection of gender, technology, and journalism and conducts research aimed at ensuring the future of news is built by diverse practitioners who understand the importance of finding and telling inclusive stories.

Lenzy Krehbiel-Burton, a Cherokee Nation citizen, is an award-winning freelance reporter based in Tulsa, Oklahoma. As of August 2019, her work also appears in the *Citizen Potawatomi Nation's Hownikan, Fairfax (Oklahoma) Chief, Journal Record, Native Oklahoma* magazine, *The New York Times, Osage News*, Reuters, *Tahlequah Daily Press*, and *Tulsa World*. A 2015 Dennis Hunt Fund fellow through the University of Southern California's Center for Health Journalism, she is on the boards of directors for both the Native American Journalists Association and the Oklahoma Pro Chapter of the Society of Professional Journalists. The two-time Oklahoma State University graduate is also a member of the Association of Health Care Journalists.

Rebecca Landsberry is the executive director of the Native American Journalists Association, which advocates for accurate representations of Indigenous people in media and press freedom throughout Indian Country. She is a former tribal media editor for the *Muscogee Nation News* and served as vice president of the Mvskoke Media Editorial Board, where she was responsible for oversight of the independent tribal agency from 2015 to 2018. She was a recipient of the National Center for American Indian Enterprise Development's Native American 40 Under 40 award in 2018. She holds a degree in journalism from the University of Oklahoma where she studied public relations and Native American studies at the Gaylord College of Journalism and Strategic Communication. She is an enrolled citizen of the Muscogee (Creek) Nation and is based in Los Angeles with deep ties to her home in Oklahoma.

Victoria LaPoe (Cherokee) is an associate professor at Ohio University's Scripps School of Journalism, focused on media inclusivity and digital media. Previously, she served as broadcasting and film coordinator and assistant professor at Western Kentucky University's School of Journalism and Broadcasting. She received her PhD from Louisiana State University in 2013. She is coauthor of *Indian Country: Telling a Story in a Digital Age; Underserved Communities and Digital Discourse: Getting Voices Heard; Resistance Advocacy as News: Digital Black Press Covers the Tea Party;* and *Oil and Water: Media Lessons from Hurricane Katrina and the Deepwater Horizon Disaster.* Victoria is vice president and education chair of the Native American Journalists Association. She has co-run the Native American Journalists Association Fellows student newsroom for the past three years.

Mia Moody-Ramirez is a professor and chair of the Baylor University Department of Journalism, Public Relations and New Media. She joined Baylor in 2001 and has maintained an active research portfolio in addition to her teaching and leadership roles. Her research emphasizes media framing of people of color, women, and other underrepresented groups. The author or coauthor of four books, Moody-Ramirez has also been widely published in a variety of academic and industry journals. She was honored with the Outstanding Woman in Journalism award by the Association for Education in Journalism and Mass Communication, and this summer received the organization's Lionel Barrow Jr. Award for Distinguished Achievement in Diversity Research and Education. She is also a 2019 fellow in the AEJMC Institute for Diverse Leadership.

Paromita Pain is an assistant professor at the University of Nevada at Reno, teaching and researching global media epistemologies. She has published widely on the intersection of gender and social media besides examining areas of online commenting, uncivil behavior, and its impact on journalistic practices. She uses qualitative and quantitative methods and has recently started focusing on computational methods of data collection and analysis. Her research has been published in refereed journals like the *Feminist Media Theory, Journalism Studies, Journalism Practice, Journalism & Mass Communication Educator, The Agenda Setting Journal,* and *Media Asia,* among others. She serves as 2019–2020 chair for the Commission on the Status of Women for AEJMC.

David D. Perlmutter is the 2019–2020 president of the Association for Education in Journalism and Mass Communication (AEJMC). He is a professor and dean of the College of Media & Communication (CoMC) at Texas Tech University. He received his BA (1985) and MA (1991) from the University of Pennsylvania and his PhD (1996) from the University of Minnesota. He is the son of two professors and so likes to think of academia as his "family business." Perlmutter has been described by the editor of *The Chronicle of Higher Education* as a "household name among American professors" because of the widespread readership of some two decades of his writings on academic careers and higher education operations for the *Chronicle* and other publications. Perlmutter is the author or editor of ten books on political communication, new media technologies, and higher education. He also published several dozen research articles for academic journals. At Louisiana State University, he edited a political communication book series and won two faculty awards including the main campus-wide award for research, teaching, and service. He has been twice elected to chair the research committee of AEJMC, one of his field's leading professional associations. In 2018, he was bestowed with the Texas Tech President's Excellence in Gender Equity Award for advancing gender diversity, inclusion, and equity in his college.

Chelsea Reynolds is an assistant professor of communications at California State University, Fullerton. She teaches courses on magazine publishing, media ethics, sexuality communication, and feature reporting. Reynolds is the recipient of numerous research awards, including the AEJMC Mary Ann Yodelis Smith Award for Feminist Scholarship. She is a former magazine writer and editor.

Nathian Shae Rodriguez is an assistant professor of digital media in the School of Journalism & Media Studies at San Diego State University and core faculty for the Area of Excellence—Digital Humanities and Global Diversity. He specializes in critical-cultural and digital media studies. His research focuses on minority representation in media, specifically LGBTQ and Latinx portrayals and identity negotiation, as well as pop culture, identity, radio broadcasting, and issues of masculinity and mascing. Rodriguez also has ten years' professional radio experience in on-air talent, sales, promotions, and social media marketing.

Marquita Smith is a former chair of AEJMC's Commission on the Status of Minorities and served on the board of directors for two years. Smith is assistant dean of the School of Journalism and New Media at the University of Mississippi. She worked in various newsrooms for sixteen years. Until June 2010, she served as Virginia Beach bureau chief at *The Virginian-Pilot*. She joined the *Pilot* as a local government editor in 2001. In 2008, Smith left the *Pilot* to complete a Knight International Journalism Fellowship in Liberia. During her year in West Africa, she created a judicial and justice reporting network and is helping journalists develop skills to cover the postwar nation's poverty reduction efforts. Before moving to Virginia, Smith worked as an assistant metro editor at the *Montgomery (AL) Advertiser*. She also has worked as a reporter at the *Lexington-Herald Leader*, the (Biloxi) *Sun Herald*, and in Knight Ridder's Washington bureau. In 2012, Smith was named as one of Journalism Degree.org's Top 50 Journalism Professors. For the 2016–2017 academic year, Smith taught as a Fulbright Scholar at the University of Ghana, Legon. Last year, she received John Brown University's Faculty Excellence Award.

www.ingramcontent.com/pod-product-compliance
Lightning Source LLC
Chambersburg PA
CBHW050652280326
41932CB00015B/2872